88665

COLLIN COUNTY COMMUNITY COLLEGE

3 1702 00209 3536

Learning Resources Center
Collin County Community College District
SPRING CREEK CAM
Plano, Texas 7507

D1308883

WITHDRAWN

HF
5548.4
R2
S3413
1999

Schicht, Gabriele.

A flying start with
SAP/R3 [i.e. SAP R/
3].

$34.95

BAKER & TAYLOR

Flying Start
with SAP R/3

Gabriele Schicht and Andrea Schmieden

 Addison-Wesley

An imprint of **Pearson Education**

Harlow, England · London · New York · Reading, Massachusetts · San Francisco · Toronto · Don Mills, Ontario · Sydney
Tokyo · Singapore · Hong Kong · Seoul · Taipei · Cape Town · Madrid · Mexico City · Amsterdam · Munich · Paris · Milan

PEARSON EDUCATION LIMITED

Head Office:
Edinburgh Gate
Harlow CM20 2JE
England
Tel: +44 (0)1279 623623
Fax: +44 (0)1279 431059
Website: www. aw.com/cseng/

London Office:
128 Long Acre
London WC2E 9AN
Tel: +44 (0)20 7447 2000
Fax: +44 (0)20 7240 5771

First published in Great Britain in 2001

© Addison-Wesley-Longman Verlag GmbH, Germany 1999

The rights of Gabriele Schicht and Andrea Schmieden to be identified as Authors of this
Work have been asserted by them in accordance with the Copyright, Designs and Patents Act 1988.

ISBN 0-201-67529-3

British Library Cataloguing-in-Publication Data
A CIP catalogue record for this book can be obtained from the British Library

Library of Congress Cataloging in Publication Data
Schicht, Gabriele.
    [SAP R/3 der schnelle Einstieg. English]
    A flying start with SAP/R3 [i.e. SAP R/3]/Gabriele Schicht and Andrea Schmieden.
        p. cm.
    Includes index.
    ISBN 0-201-67529-3 (pbk.)
    1. SAP R/3. 2. Business enterprises--Computer networks--Management. I. Schmieden,
Andrea. II. Title.

    HF5548.4.R2 S3413 2000
    650'.0285'53769--dc21

                                                                    00-058915

All rights reserved; no part of this publication may be reproduced, stored in a retrieval system,
or transmitted in any form or by any means, electronic, mechanical, photocopying, recording, or
otherwise without either the prior written permission of the Publishers or a licence permitting
restricted copying in the United Kingdom issued by the Copyright Licensing Agency Ltd,
90 Tottenham Court Road, London W1P 0LP. This book may not be lent, resold, hired out or
otherwise disposed of by way of trade in any form of binding or cover other than that in which it is
published, without the prior consent of the Publishers.

The programs in this book have been included for their instructional value. The publisher does not
offer any warranties or representations in respect of their fitness for a particular purpose,
nor does the publisher accept any liability for any loss or damage arising from their use.

Many of the designations used by manufacturers and sellers to distinguish their
products are claimed as trademarks. Pearson Education Limited has made every
attempt to supply trademark information about manufacturers and their products mentioned
in this book. A list of tademark designations and their owners appears on this page.

Trademark Notice
Windows 95, 98 and NT are trademarks of the Microsoft Corporation.

10 9 8 7 6 5 4 3 2 1

Designed by Claire Brodman, Book Designs.
Typeset by Pantek Arts Ltd, Maidstone, Kent.
Printed and bound in Italy.

The Publishers' policy is to use paper manufactured from sustainable forests.

Contents

About this book

WHO SHOULD READ THIS BOOK?

This book is intended for all those who answer 'Yes' to one of the following questions:

- Are you a newcomer to SAP R/3?
- Do you have experience with SAP R/3, but now want to know how to use it more efficiently?
- Do you want to prepare yourself in advance for working with SAP R/3?

Training
The book can also be used in training sessions as course material. The examples presented are largely derived from the Human Resources (HR) module, and can be reconstructed with the help of the demonstration and training system IDES.

HOW SHOULD YOU WORK WITH THIS BOOK?

You need no previous knowledge at all for this book. The best way is to work through it step by step. When a section is not essential for understanding what follows and can therefore be skipped, it is marked accordingly.

You'll certainly find it easier to memorize what you read if you reconstruct the examples on your computer. But thanks to the many illustrations, the examples are easy to follow even without access to SAP R/3.

The book deals with SAP R/3 Release 4.0 and Release 4.5.

Acknowledgements

Many thanks to the following (in alphabetical order) for their support: Prof. Sissi Closs (Comet Communication GmbH), Bernhard Hochlehnert (SAP AG), Hanno Holzheuser (SAP AG), Gabriele John (SAP AG), Margret Klein-Magar (SAP AG), Gerald Koehn (SAP AG), Leif Jensen-Pistorius (SAP AG), Verena Müller, Katherine Totten (SAP AG), Tomas Wehren (Addison Wesley Longman).

CHAPTER 1

What is SAP R/3?

SAP R/3 is standard business solution software, which supports organizations in business processes such as invoicing, warehouse management and Human Resources. SAP R/3 is used worldwide by organizations in many sectors of industry.

SAP is the company's name, and stands for *Systems, Applications and Products in Data Processing*. The 'R' in R/3 stands for *Real-time* and means that data is updated immediately, so that it is available for further processing by any user. The '3' indicates that this is the third generation of the product. 4.0 and 4.5 indicate the release or version number.

1.1 WHAT'S SPECIAL ABOUT SAP R/3?

The individual departments of an organization usually have differing DP requirements. This often means that each department applies its own DP solutions. The result is group-constrained solutions: isolated applications and datasets, which are not connected to one another. To make one department's accrued data available to others, interfaces between the systems have to be implemented and maintained, or data has to be entered more than once. This costs time and money, and is prone to errors.

As markets become tighter, businesses depend more than ever on being able to maintain up-to-date reliable data that they can evaluate and process. SAP R/3 enables them to do exactly that.

Integration

With SAP R/3, a company's entire business data is integrated in a single system. The data is entered only once, and is immediately available to all of the other departments of the company for further processing and evaluation. All departments can access the current data at any time.

Client–server architecture

In the client–server architecture, only part of the processing takes place directly on the workstation computers – the clients. Central computers – the servers – supply other services such as data storage. This enables all users to access the same data, so that the individual computers can be utilized optimally. SAP R/3 uses a three-tier client–server architecture (Figure 1.1). It allows the data retention database, the applications, and the processing of user inputs to run on different computers. One of the advantages of this architecture is that the computers can be distributed across a number of different sites. This is especially important for companies with several business locations or international activities.

Scalability

A further advantage of the three-tier client–server architecture is better scalability – customizing the system to the size of the company. SAP R/3 is suitable for large corporations as well as small and medium-sized businesses.

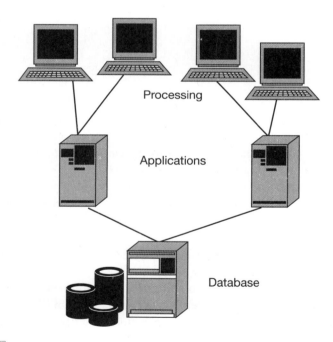

FIGURE 1.1   Three-tier client–server architecture. Copyright © SAP AG

Standard
software

SAP R/3 is standard business software, which offers companies a comprehensive range of functions to support their business processes. By using this standard software a company is spared the time-consuming in-house development of this extensive functional range, and can profit from SAP's many years of experience in thousands of installations. In comparison to individual solutions, there will also be a reduction in the regular costs for maintenance, and for adapting software to new requirements such as the changeover to the euro.

Customizing

In spite of standardization there are particular facts that must be taken into account in every organization. Company-specific defaults and processing rules can be set in SAP R/3 for this purpose. This is known as *Customizing*. In addition, SAP R/3 provides a development environment with which a company can program its own enhancements and customizations.

CHAPTER 2

The first step: SAP R/3 logon

Before you can work with SAP R/3, you have to execute a SAP R/3 logon. System administration gives you a user name and password for this.

During logon, the user name and the password are used to check whether you have access rights to SAP R/3, and which functions are available to you. This protects the company data from unauthorized access.

2.1   LOGGING ON

Prerequisites

Before you can log on, the following prerequisites must be satisfied:

- Your computer has been set up for working with SAP R/3. The SAP R/3 graphical user interface (*SAPGUI – SAP Graphical User Interface*) is installed and the computer is connected to a SAP R/3 server via the intranet.

- You have been given a user name and password by the system administration.

- You know which *client* you must specify.

Client

When you log on, you must specify which client you want. A client is a closed unit within a SAP R/3 system. There is one client number for each client. Client numbers can be used in corporate groups, for instance, to identify the various companies in the group.

There is often also a client for training and practice. If you specify the relevant client number when logging on, you can practise with the demo data. This demo data is completely separate from the 'real' data used in production operation.

You can start SAP R/3 on different computers with different operating systems. The examples in this book relate to Windows 95, Windows 98 and Windows NT, but calling SAP R/3 from a different operating system is similar.

The screen shots you'll find in this book are from the SAP training system IDES (*International Demo and Education System*). If IDES is also in use in your firm, you can follow the examples directly in IDES. Ask your system administrator for details about the IDES logon. If you don't have access to IDES, be sure to use the training client number when practising, so that your practice data is not transferred into production operation.

How to log on

1 Call SAP R/3. Do this by double-clicking on the SAP R/3 symbol on your Windows desktop.

If you don't see that symbol on your Windows desktop, you can also call SAP R/3 from the Windows Start menu. Click on **Start** (START) in the lower left corner of the screen, point to PROGRAMS, and then click on SAP R/3.

The SAP R/3 logon window will be displayed (Figure 2.1).

2 Enter the client you want in the 'Client' field. While practising with this book you should enter the training client number. The system administrator will give you this number.

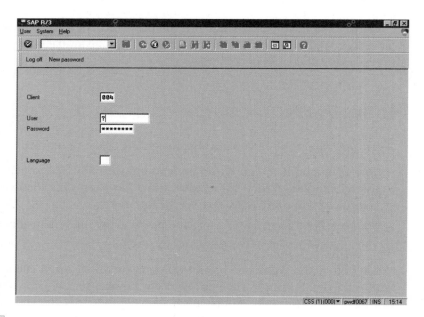

FIGURE 2.1 SAP R/3 logon window

TIP IF YOU CANNOT FIND THE SAP R/3 SYMBOL OR THE MENU FUNCTION...

If you can't find the SAP R/3 Symbol or the menu function, the reason may be one of the following:

■ A different symbol or name is used in your organization.

■ The SAP R/3 user interface is not installed on your computer.

Consult the relevant system administrator in your organization.

3   If the cursor is not yet at the beginning of the 'User' field, press the tab key (Tab). This key always takes you to the next field.

4   In the 'User' field, enter the user name the system administrator gave you. This is usually a short code or a number, set by the system administration according to specific rules.

5   Press the tab key (Tab) again to set the cursor in the 'Password' field.

6   Enter the password the system administrator gave you. For security reasons, the characters you enter are not displayed.

7   Enter the language code 'EN' in the 'Language' field. This causes windows, menus and fields to be displayed in English. If you want to choose a different language, enter the language code of your choice, e.g. 'FR' for French. If you prefer, you can select the language you usually want to work in later. Therefore, you can leave the 'Language' field blank when logging on. You'll find out more about this in Chapter 16.

8   Press the input key (Return).

How to change your password

When you log on for the first time, you must change the password. A dialog box is displayed automatically for this in the initial logon (Figure 2.2).

1   Decide your personal password, and then enter it.

TIP WHEN IS YOUR PASSWORD SECURE?

Your password has a similar function to the PIN (personal identification number) for an ATM (automated teller machine) card – it protects the company data from unauthorized access. It is therefore essential to keep it secret. Avoid passwords that are easy to guess, such as your name or date of birth. And remember: even the cleverest password is of no use if it is on a piece of paper on your desk! So don't write down your password, or keep the note in a safe place. You'll find more tips on passwords in the section 'Changing your password' later.

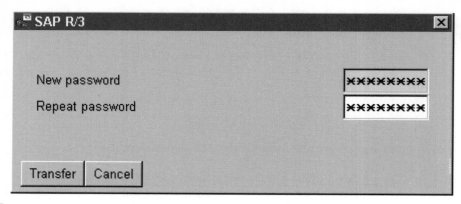

FIGURE 2.2   New password

2   Press the (Tab) key – not the (Return) key. To make sure that you have not mistyped it, you must enter it a second time. Move the cursor into the 'Repeat password' field with the (Tab) key to do this.

Make a mental note of this password: you have to enter it every time you log on.

3   Click on TRANSFER.

A copyright notice is displayed.

4   Click on CONTINUE after you have read the notice.

You have successfully logged on to the SAP R/3 System, and your screen looks something like Figure 2.3.

2.2   LOGGING OFF

When you want to stop working with SAP R/3, log off. This is possible in any SAP R/3 window. You should also log off if you leave your workstation, to prevent unauthorized persons accessing the system. If your computer is equipped with a screen saver with password protection, you can also activate this when you leave your workstation briefly.

How to log off

1   Choose SYSTEM | LOG OFF in the menu bar.

The message shown in Figure 2.4 is displayed.

This message is displayed even if you haven't entered or changed any data.

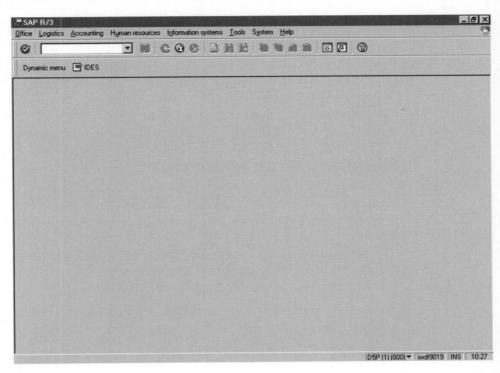

FIGURE 2.3   SAP R/3 after successful logon

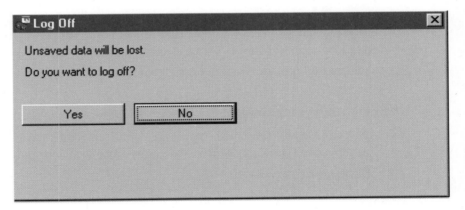

FIGURE 2.4   Message preceding logoff

To prevent an accidental logoff, the NO button is selected as default. You can see this from the dark border.

2 Click on YES.

If you are using the keyboard, press the tab key (Tab) to choose the YES button, and then press (Return).

You have now logged off and left SAP R/3.

2.3   CHANGING YOUR PASSWORD

For security reasons, system administration can decide that you must change your password at regular intervals, e.g. every month. When it's time, you'll be notified about it.

However, you can also change your password earlier. One change per day is possible. The five last used passwords are not permissible.

Rules for passwords

Follow these rules when deciding on your password:

- In general, a password must consist of at least three characters, and may not be longer than eight characters. However, your system administrator may have set other defaults.

- Permissible characters are letters, digits and punctuation marks such as dot and comma.

- The password may not begin with a question mark, exclamation mark or three identical characters. Furthermore, the password may not contain three successive characters that also occur in your user name. For example, if your user name is MILLER, you cannot choose BELLE as your password.

- No distinction is made between upper and lower case.

How to change your password

1 Enter the client, your user name and your current password in the logon window (see Figure 2.1). Move to each successive field with the (Tab) key.

2 Click on NEW PASSWORD.

The dialog box for entering a new password is displayed (Figure 2.5).

3 Enter your chosen password.

The five last used passwords are not permissible.

4 Press the (Tab) key and repeat the new password.

5 Click on TRANSFER.

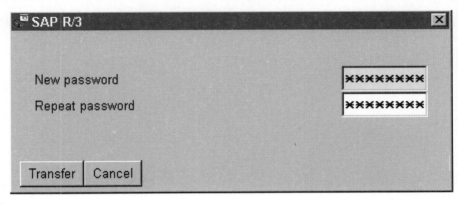

FIGURE 2.5   Change password

TIP   **DID YOU FORGET YOUR PASSWORD?**

If you forgot your password, you must consult system administration. They cannot find out your old password, but they will give you the password that was given to you for the initial logon, to let you log on again. After logging on, you must change the password again immediately.

CHAPTER 3

A short tour of the SAP R/3 user interface

In the previous chapter, you learned how to log on to SAP R/3. In doing this, you have already used the SAP R/3 user interface.

User interface

We employ the term user interface to denote the windows, menus, fields and so on that are available for controlling a computer application.

Follow us now on a short tour, in which you will meet the individual elements of the SAP R/3 user interface.

3.1 WINDOWS

In SAP R/3 you normally work in windows. An example of such a window is the Logon window, which you already know (Figure 3.1). All SAP R/3 windows are similar in layout.

3.1.1 Title bar

The title bar is used for orientation, and shows the name of the displayed window. It also contains the usual Windows symbols for changing the window size, and for closing the window:

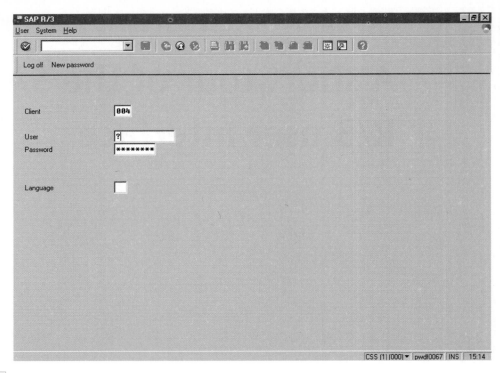

FIGURE 3.1   Layout of a SAP R/3 window, using the Logon window as an example

■ With the ▬ (MINIMIZE) button, you make the window into an icon. It is then shown as a symbol in the Windows taskbar. If you want to display the window in its original size, click on this symbol in the taskbar.

■ With the ☐ (MAXIMIZE) button, you expand the window to full screen size. This can be a good idea if you are working only with SAP R/3 and don't want to be distracted by other applications displayed in the background. When you have maximized the window, its title bar will display the ⬚ (RESTORE WINDOW) button instead of the MAXIMIZE button.

■ With the ⬚ (RESTORE WINDOW) button, you shrink a maximized window back to the original size. If other windows are open, they become visible again. This setting is appropriate if you want to keep an eye on information from other applications while you are working in the SAP R/3 window. If you want to switch to the window of a different application, simply click on the window you want. After you have clicked on the ⬚ button, you will see the ☐ button in the window title bar once more.

■ With the ☒ (CLOSE) button, you close the window. If only one window was open, this is equivalent to a logoff from SAP R/3. To prevent an accidental logoff, a query about this appears beforehand, and you can say whether you are really logging off or want to go on working.

3.1.2   Menu bar and standard toolbars

Menu bar

The menu bar contains menus from which you can select SAP R/3 functions. You will learn more about this in Chapter 4.

At the right-hand edge of the menu bar you will see a colour palette symbol. This symbol lets you display a menu whose functions allow you, for example, to specify the screen display colours and make other settings. You will find more information on this in Chapter 17.

Standard toolbar

The standard toolbar enables you to execute frequently required functions, quickly and simply. All you have to do is click on the corresponding symbol. You can also execute the functions via the menu bar or key combinations. However, the standard toolbar is the fastest and simplest method.

The standard toolbar contains symbols for functions that are needed in all application areas, such as (SAVE) or (PRINT), so they are the same in all SAP R/3 windows. You will become familiar with the meanings of the individual symbols in subsequent chapters. You will also find an overview and short description of the symbols in the Appendix.

TIP   WHICH FUNCTION IS CALLED?

If you want to know which function is called by a particular symbol, move the mouse pointer to the symbol without clicking on it. After a moment a short explanation of the symbol appears. You will also see which key combination could be used to call this function.

Quick info

This quick way of displaying information about a symbol is also called 'Quick info'. Figure 3.2 shows an example.

FIGURE 3.2   Quick info in the Logon window

Command field

The command field is integrated into the standard toolbar. You can enter transaction codes here, for example. You will find out more about that in Chapter 9.

Greyed symbols

Some functions cannot be executed in every situation. In this case the corresponding symbol is shown in grey. Not many functions are available to you before you are logged on. This is why most of the symbols in Figure 3.2 are greyed.

Button bar

Below the standard toolbar you will see the *button bar*. Sometimes this is called the application toolbar. Just like symbols, buttons are used for fast access to functions. Buttons can be labelled (see Figure 3.2) or given an image, or sometimes both. Which buttons are displayed depends on the chosen application area.

3.1.3 Fields

Input fields

You came across input fields when logging on. Input fields are labelled fields into which you enter data. The next chapters tell you how to fill in such fields. You will also see some other types of fields.

Required entry fields

Did you notice the question mark in the 'User' field in the Logon window (see Figure 3.1)? This is how fields that must be filled in are marked.

3.1.4 Status bar

Short messages and activity data are displayed in the status bar on the lower edge of the window.

TIP | **IS THE STATUS BAR DISPLAYED?**

If the status bar is not displayed on your screen, it is hidden. You will learn in Chapter 17 how to display the status bar again.

Messages

Messages are displayed on the left in the status bar. A prefix letter indicates the type of message:

Letter	Message type	Description
S	Success message	Displayed when a function has been successfully executed.
W	Warning	Displayed when the data may possibly be faulty. However, processing can continue in spite of the warning.
E	Error	Displayed when a missing or incorrect entry means that processing cannot continue.

Figure 3.3 shows an example of an error message.

E: Name or password is incorrect. Please re-enter   CSS (1) (001) ▼ | pawdf044 | INS | 19:06

FIGURE 3.3   Error message in the status bar

TIP   **DO YOU WANT TO DISPLAY MESSAGES IN A SEPARATE MESSAGE WINDOW?**

Messages in the status bar are easily overlooked. If an error message is displayed in the status bar, you cannot continue your work until the error situation is rectified. But if you have overlooked the error message, you may wonder why you cannot continue.

There is a simple remedy here: You can choose to have messages displayed in a separate message window as well, or have an alert tone sounded for error messages. You will find out more about that in Chapter 17.

Figure 3.4 shows an error message in a message window.

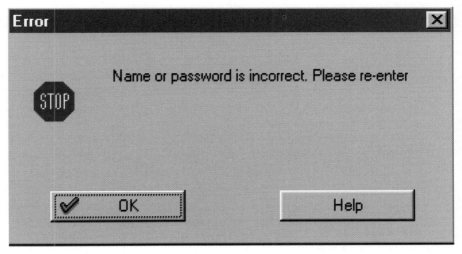

FIGURE 3.4   Not so easily overlooked – Error message in message window

The following message types can also be displayed in a message window:

Letter	Message type	Description
I	Information	Displayed when the message is for information only.
A	Abnormal end	Displayed after a serious error occurs. The active application is terminated.

SPRING CREEK CAMPUS

As well as messages, the status bar displays further information on the right (Figure 3.5).

| D5P (1) (000) ▼ | iwdf9019 | INS | 15:45 |

FIGURE 3.5   Status bar

SAP R/3 system

In the first of the four fields in the status bar you can see the name of the SAP R/3 system to which you have logged on.

Session

The system display is followed by the session number in brackets. You can open several sessions in SAP R/3. You will find information on this in Chapter 4.

Client

The session display is followed by the client number in brackets, as you gave it when you logged on.

Server name

In the second display field in the status bar you can see the server to which you are currently connected. This information can be of interest for system administration in certain situations. Depending on how SAP R/3 is set up in your organization, you may be connected to a different server each time the graphical user interface is started. This depends on the load on the various servers.

Insert/ Overwrite

In the third field of the status bar you can determine whether the data you enter will overwrite the existing data, or whether it will be inserted. The abbreviation INS stands for insert. OVW stands for overwrite. To switch between insert and overwrite, simply click on the corresponding display in the status bar. You can also press the (Insert) key on your keyboard.

Time of day/ Response time

In the fourth field the current time is normally displayed. However, you can choose to have the system response time displayed. To switch between time of day and response time, simply click on the displayed time in the status bar.

At a glance

If you want to see the activity data at a glance, click on the small downward triangle in the first field of the status bar. This causes a menu to be displayed, showing further activity data. You can see an example in Figure 3.6.

Set display

By clicking on the menu entries you can change the display in the status bar. Just give it a try, and select the data that is most useful for your work. We will come back to this data at a later stage.

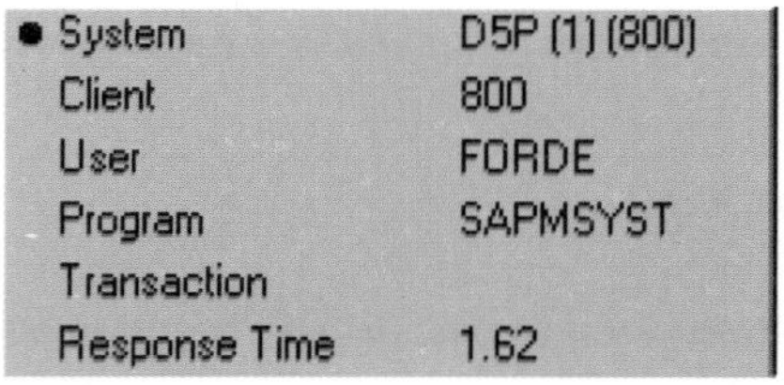

● System	D5P (1) (800)
Client	800
User	FORDE
Program	SAPMSYST
Transaction	
Response Time	1.62

FIGURE 3.6   Activity data at a glance

3.2   DIALOG BOXES

Sometimes further details are needed for processing the input data. In these cases a dialog box is displayed, in which you can enter the necessary information (Figure 3.7).

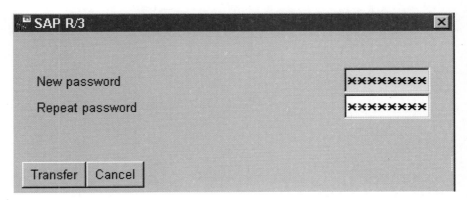

FIGURE 3.7   Example of a dialog box

Dialog boxes are displayed in front of the main window. The dialog box becomes the active window, and you can only continue working in the main window after providing the necessary inputs in the dialog box.

You can move a dialog box on the screen, but not make it into an icon or expand it to full screen size.

You will learn about other dialog boxes in subsequent chapters.

CHAPTER 4

Navigation: How to move around in SAP R/3

You've already coped successfully with the first steps in SAP R/3. Now we want to study it all in more detail. This will give you greater confidence in dealing with SAP R/3.

First we will take another look at the menus.

4.1   MENUS – WHERE TO FIND WHAT YOU WANT

Let's assume you are employed in the HR department in your company. The HR department is subdivided into several application areas and task areas. Imagine you are responsible for the initial entry of applicant data in Recruitment.

These application areas and task areas are reflected in the SAP R/3 menu structure. To reach the functions you need for processing your tasks, simply go through the menus until you find the relevant point.

How to work with menus

1   Log on again as we did in Chapter 2. You'll see the start window once more (Figure 4.1).

Directly after logon, the menu bar shows the application areas that you can choose, e.g. HUMAN RESOURCES.

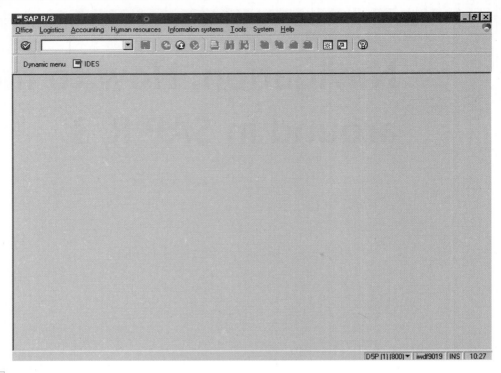

FIGURE 4.1 Main menu level

You also see the standard menus SYSTEM and HELP, which are displayed in every window. The SYSTEM menu enables you to call system functions such as LOG OFF. You will learn about some of these functions in later chapters. The HELP menu provides entry to the SAP R/3 help functions. You will find out more about this in Chapter 8.

The menu level that you see directly after logging on is known as the main menu level or SAP menu.

2 Now click on the HUMAN RESOURCES menu.

The menu is expanded and you can see the options it contains (Figure 4.2).

A small triangle to the right of a menu option shows that it is a cascading menu. When you point the mouse to a cascading menu like this, the subordinate menu options are displayed.

3 Point to the cascading menu for PERSONNEL MANAGEMENT, and click on the menu option RECRUITMENT, to choose the application area Recruitment (Figure 4.3).

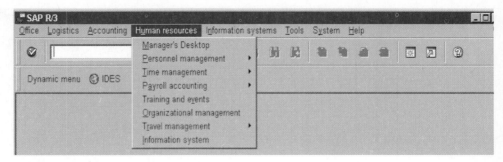

FIGURE 4.2   Menu options in the HUMAN RESOURCES menu

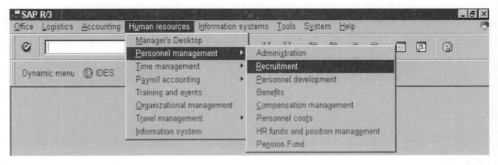

FIGURE 4.3   Choose the application area Recruitment

TIP   ABBREVIATED NOTATION

Since at this stage you are choosing a menu option for the first time, we have described the individual steps in great detail. However, you will soon become familiar with this procedure, so that we can represent the individual steps more briefly. Instead of going through each of the menus and cascades, we shall simply say 'Choose HUMAN RESOURCES | PERSONNEL MANAGEMENT | RECRUITMENT'.

After you have chosen the application area Recruitment, the menu and button bars change. You can now call this area's applications from the menu bar or button bar (Figure 4.4).

4   Now choose APPLICANT MASTER DATA | INITIAL ENTRY OF BASIC DATA, or simply click in the button bar on INITIAL DATA ENTRY, to choose the application for initial entry of applicant data (Figure 4.5).

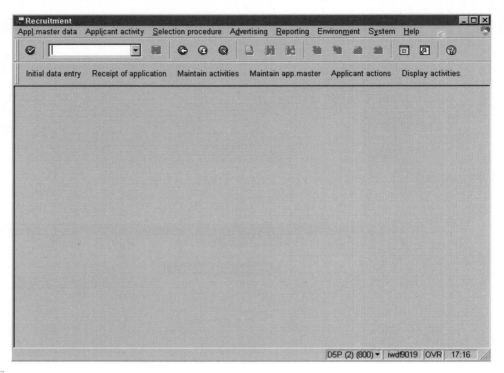

FIGURE 4.4   You can choose applications here

TIP WOULD YOU RATHER WORK WITH THE KEYBOARD?

Naturally you can also choose menus and menu options via the keyboard:

1. Press (F10) to activate menu choice via keyboard. The first menu is selected.

2. Use the (right arrow) and (left arrow) keys to move the selection to the menu you want, and press (Return).

3. Use the (arrow up) and (arrow down) keys to move the selection to the menu option you want, and press (Return).

It's even quicker with key combinations: For instance, if you want to choose the menu APPLI-CANT MASTER DATA, press (Alt) + (A). You always know which key you should press along with (Alt) by the underlined letter in the menu name. To choose HUMAN RESOURCES | PER-SONNEL MANAGEMENT | RECRUITMENT via the keyboard, for instance, press (Alt) + (H), hold the (Alt) key down and then press (P) followed by (R).

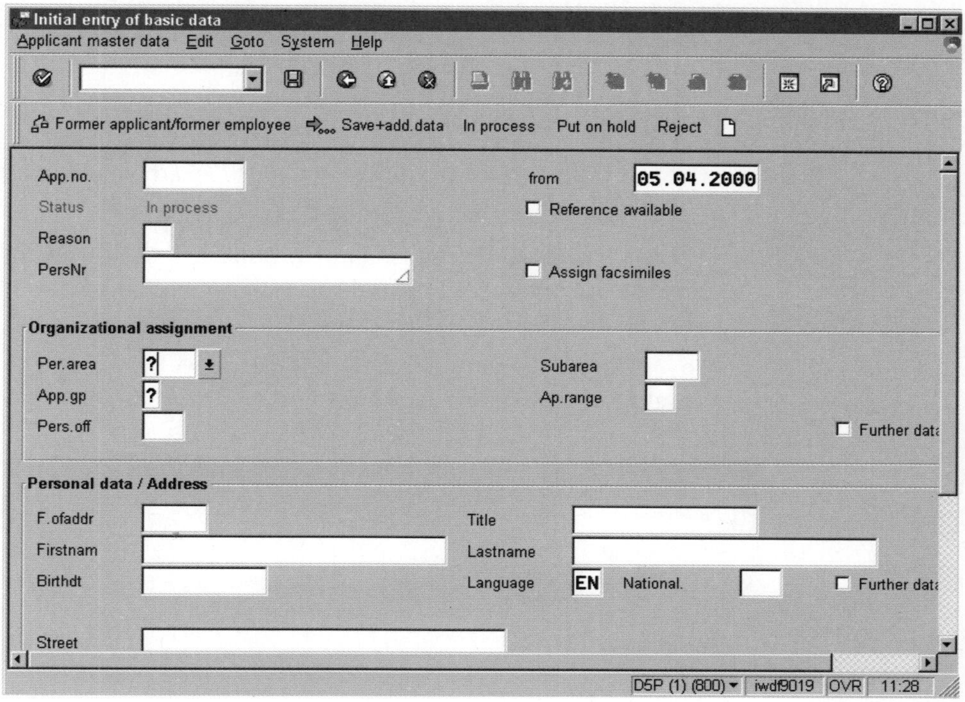

FIGURE 4.5 Window for initial entry of applicant data

TIP   **AND IF YOU ARE USING THE KEYBOARD**

You can also choose options in the button bar through the keyboard.

1. Press the tab key (Tab) until the required option is selected.
2. Press (Return).

Now you have reached the right place for entering data. You will learn more about that in the next chapter. We would like to ask you to be patient a little longer, though. We still have a few tips on navigation in SAP R/3 for you.

4.2   THE DYNAMIC MENU – ALL MENUS AT A GLANCE

Dynamic menu

The SAP R/3 menu structure is fairly extensive – hardly surprising with such a powerful system. If you want to gain an overview of the menu structure, the *Dynamic menu* will help you. The dynamic menu shows all menus and their options in an expanding structure similar to Windows Explorer. You can call applications directly from the dynamic menu.

How to use the dynamic menu

1   Click on ⚓ (EXIT), until you see the SAP R/3 start window again (cf. Figure 4.1).

2   Click in the button bar on DYNAMIC MENU.

The top level of the menu structure is displayed. Options marked with a ⊞ have subordinate options. You can display the subordinate items by clicking on the ⊞ or double-clicking on the option.

3   For instance, display the application that we just called from the menu. It should look similar to Figure 4.6.

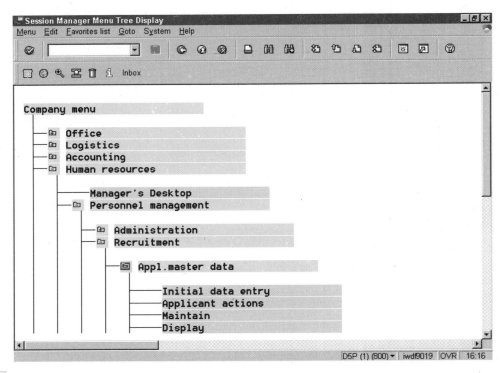

FIGURE 4.6   How the dynamic menu shows the menu structure

4   You can start the application directly from this view with a double click on the option 'Initial data entry'.

5   Click on ⚓ again until you see the SAP R/3 start window.

KEY COMBINATIONS – AN ALTERNATIVE TO MENUS

You can also call frequently used functions in SAP R/3 with the function keys on your keyboard. If you work regularly with SAP R/3 you may find it easier and quicker to operate with function keys than with menu functions. But there is no need to memorize the keys. All functions are also available from the menus.

You can find out which functions you can call with function keys in a given situation as follows:

How to display the available function keys and key combinations

1   Click with the right mouse button in the work area of the window, or press (Ctrl) + (F).

A menu of the available functions and associated function keys is displayed Figure 4.7).

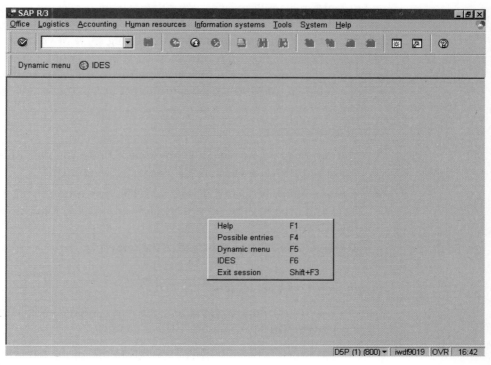

FIGURE 4.7   Function keys for the SAP R/3 start window

2   Click on an empty space outside the menu to close it again.

TIP   **DOES YOUR KEYBOARD HAVE ONLY 12 FUNCTION KEYS?**

24 function keys are assigned in SAP R/3: (F1) to (F24). However, a standard PC keyboard has only 12 function keys. To call functions (F13) to (F24), use function keys (F1) to (F12) in combination with the shift key. For example, you would call function (F13) by pressing (Shift) + (F1). It is easy to remember this if you think of the time: 15.00 corresponds to 3 p.m., and you reach (F15) with (Shift) + (F3).

4.4   JUGGLING WITH WINDOWS – WORKING WITH MULTIPLE SESSIONS

Session

Normally you work with just one SAP R/3 window, as you have seen so far. Such a window is also called a *Session*. The first session is opened after logon.

Sometimes it can be useful to open additional sessions. For example, imagine you are busy entering applicant data. Your line manager calls and wants you to create a report for her. If you only had one session at your disposal, either you would have to stop the entry of applicant data – possibly losing some of your previous inputs – or you would have to make your line manager wait – also not a good alternative. It is better to open a further session for creating the report. Your work so far in the first session is retained, and you can execute another task in the second session.

Additional sessions

How to open a session

1   You can open a new session at any time. Choose the menu function SYSTEM | CREATE SESSION, or click on 🗐 (CREATE NEW SESSION).

2   A new window is opened (Figure 4.8). The new window shows the main menu level and becomes the current window. Inputs you make now are effective in this window.

The session number is displayed in the status bar.

How to switch between sessions

■ If you want to continue working in a different session, simply click in the window you want. This then becomes the current window.

You can also switch between different sessions in one of the following ways. They are particularly convenient if you have expanded the current window to the full screen size:

■ Press (Alt) + (Tab).

■ Click on the symbol of the required session in the Windows taskbar.

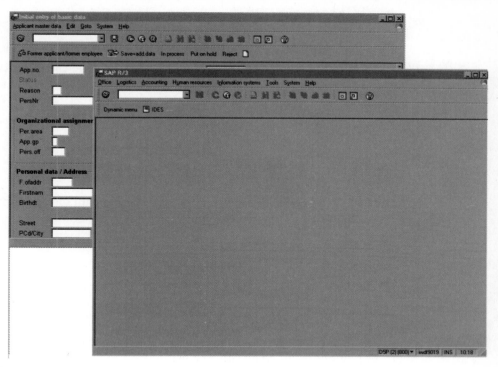

FIGURE 4.8   Two sessions

How to close an additional session

1   Switch to the session you want to close.

TIP   **DO YOU WANT TO SAVE CHANGES?**

When closing an additional session, SAP R/3 complies with your request at once – the session is closed, even if data could be lost in the process. So if you want to save changes to the data, you must do so before closing the session. You will learn more about this in Chapter 7.

---

2   Exit the session in one of the following ways:

- Choose SYSTEM | END SESSION in the menu bar.
- Click on **X** in the upper right corner of the window.
- Press (Alt) + (F4).

How to close the last session

1 To close the last session, you can proceed as for closing an additional session.

However, closing the last session is equivalent to logging off from SAP R/3. So, just as when logging off, you are asked whether you really want to log off.

2 As you have not input any data yet, you are free to log off.

4.5   **BACK, EXIT, CANCEL – SUBTLE DIFFERENCES**

Now a few tips about the standard toolbar. The standard toolbar displays the following symbols, with which you can quit a window or application:

⬅ BACK

⬆ EXIT (LOG OFF/EXIT SESSION)

❌ CANCEL

There are subtle differences between the individual functions, and we want to examine these.

The function of ⬅ (BACK) depends on the window in which it is called.

Initial window

In SAP R/3, many applications consist of several windows, which you fill in one after another. The first of these windows is often called the *Initial window* or initial screen. If you click on BACK in one of these initial windows, the window with the menu for the application area is displayed again.

Detail window

The windows following the initial window are referred to as *Detail windows* or detail screens. If you click on BACK in a detail window, the initial window is displayed again. You will see an example of this later.

If data would be lost, a message to this effect is displayed and you can save the data beforehand.

The ⬆ (EXIT) symbol terminates the current application and displays the previous menu level or the main menu level.

In the logon window (see Figure 2.1) there is no previous menu level. So in this case the symbol has the same effect as the menu function SYSTEM | LOG OFF.

Similarly, when you are at main menu level (see Figure 2.3) there is no previous menu level. So in this case the session is terminated when you click on ⬆. If it was the last session, this again corresponds to logoff.

With ❌ (CANCEL), you can cancel the current application without saving the data. If you click on CANCEL in an initial window, the window with the menu for the application area is displayed again. From a detail window you return to the initial window. Even if the cancellation will result in data losses, no confirmation prompt is displayed. You will see an example of this also.

TIP   WHAT WILL HAPPEN?

If you're not completely sure what will happen when you click on 🔼, simply display the quick info text for the symbol. Remember this? Point the mouse at the symbol without clicking. You will then see whether the symbol has the function EXIT, LOG OFF or EXIT SESSION.

4.6   EVERYTHING IN VIEW – SCROLLING IN A WINDOW

Sometimes the contents of a window cannot be fully displayed, because the contents do not fit into the window. They are either too long or too wide, or both. The window then automatically acquires a scroll bar on the right or lower edge for the relevant direction (Figure 4.9).

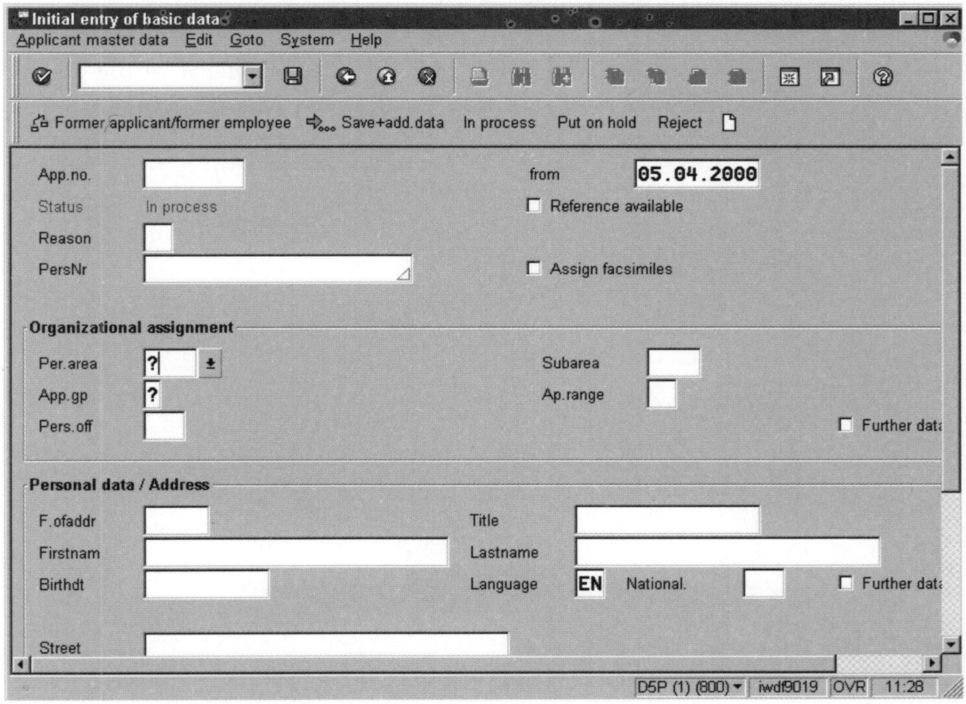

FIGURE 4.9   The INITIAL ENTRY OF BASIC DATA window with two scroll bars

You can now scroll in various ways to see the contents:

Scrolling with the mouse
■ You can move the slider box with the mouse and thus scroll to the position you want. You can scroll up or down with the vertical scroll bar, and right or left with the horizontal.

Scrolling line by line
■ If you want to scroll line by line, click on the scroll arrow in the required direction, e.g. ▼. However, it's quicker to scroll with the slider box.

Scrolling page by page
■ If you want to page forward or backward, press the (Page Up) or (Page Down) key on the keyboard.

Scrolling to a particular point
■ You can also click on the grey area between the slider box and the scroll arrow. This will bring you to wherever you want to be.

TIP   **WHAT'S FASTEST?**

When you are scrolling, data often has to be reloaded over the network. This means that screen or page scrolling is generally faster than line by line, which would require more frequent reloading.

In this chapter you have extended your knowledge of the graphical user interface. You are now well equipped for the next chapter, where you'll learn to deal with applications.

CHAPTER 5

Here we go: The first application

You will often input data when working with SAP R/3. Whether you are issuing an invoice, ordering material or entering personnel data, what all these business processes have in common is data entry.

Imagine you work in the HR department in your company. All incoming job applications land on your desk, and you are responsible for the initial entry of the applicant data. This is where the SAP R/3 HR (*Human Resources*) module comes in.

If this module is not used in your company or you do not have access rights to it, you can easily follow the examples with the help of the illustrations. The examples do not assume any previous knowledge of HR management, and you will have no difficulty in transferring what you learn to your application area.

5.1   STARTING THE RIGHT APPLICATION

The first step towards entering your data is to start the right application.

How to start an application

1   Log on as you learned in Chapter 2.

2   In the start window (see Figure 2.3) choose HUMAN RESOURCES | PERSONNEL MANAGEMENT | RECRUITMENT once more.

The RECRUITMENT window is displayed (Figure 5.1).

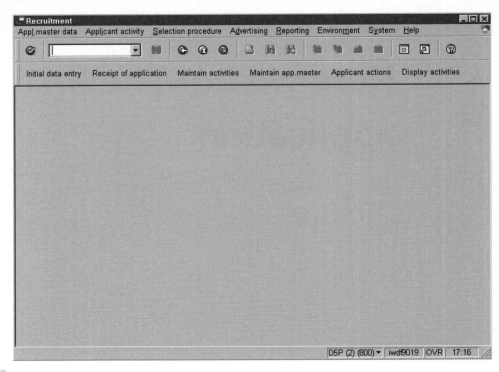

FIGURE 5.1   RECRUITMENT window

3   Click in the button bar on INITIAL DATA ENTRY.

The INITIAL ENTRY OF BASIC DATA window is displayed (Figure 5.2).

TIP   **DOES THE WINDOW ON YOUR SCREEN LOOK DIFFERENT?**

If the window on your screen looks different, it has been specially customized for your company. For example, your screen can show extra fields or differently named ones.

5.2   **MOVING THE CURSOR**

You have now displayed the window for the initial entry of applicant data and can begin to input data.

Cursor

After the window is opened, the cursor blinks in 'Per.area' for input of the personnel area. If you now input data via the keyboard, it will be inserted in this field.

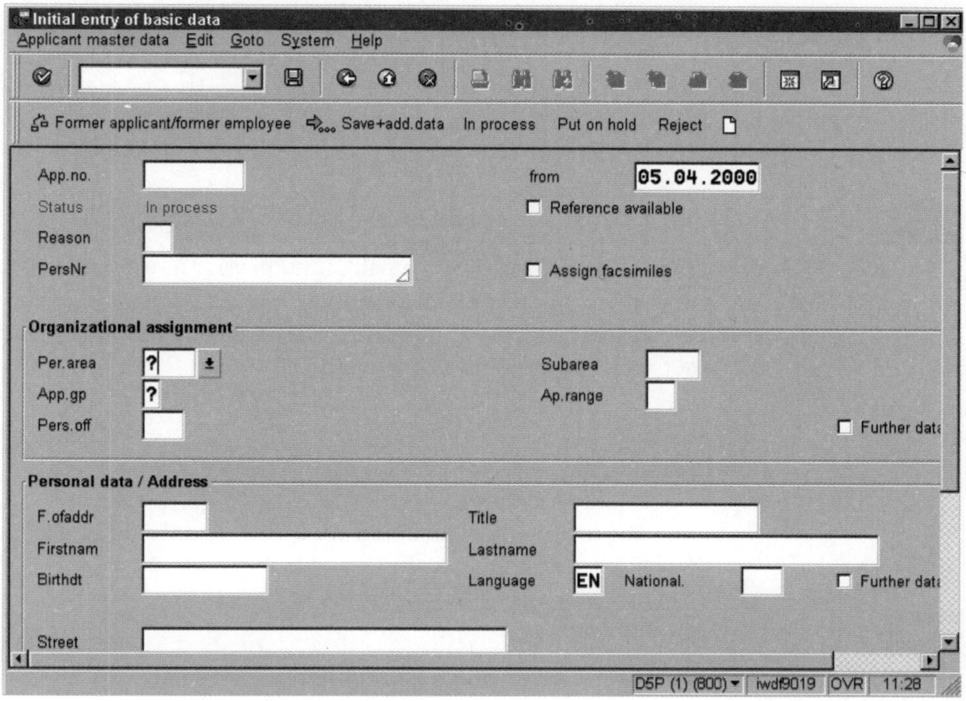

FIGURE 5.2   Window for initial entry of applicant data

However, suppose you want to enter an applicant's name and address first. In this case you first have to move the cursor to the appropriate field. You can do this with the keyboard or the mouse.

How to set the cursor in a field

▨ Press the tab key (Tab) to advance the cursor one field. Press the tab key until the cursor is in the 'First name' field.

▨ If you'd rather use the mouse, simply click in the 'First name' field. The cursor is then positioned in this field.

TIP   JUMPED TOO FAR?

If you have jumped too far, you can move the cursor one field back again with (Shift) + (Tab).

5.3 ENTERING DATA

When the cursor is in the correct field, you can enter the data. In the example below, we enter an applicant's name, address and date of birth.

TIP DOES THE CURSOR JUMP ON AT THE END OF THE FIELD?

When the cursor reaches the end of the field, it normally advances automatically to the next field. This is especially handy if you are entering a lot of data. If the cursor on your computer is not advancing automatically, you can alter this very easily by changing the relevant settings. You will find out more about this in Chapter 17.

How to input data

1 Enter the first name of an applicant in the field 'First name'.

TIP DID YOU TYPE DATA INCORRECTLY?

If you typed data incorrectly, you can delete the incorrect data with the (Backspace) key or with (Delete). (Backspace) deletes the character to the left of the cursor. (Delete) deletes the character to the right of the cursor. If you want to enter something at a particular point in a field, move the cursor to the right or left with the keyboard arrow keys (Arrow r) and (Arrow l) until you reach the required point.

2 Move the cursor on, and enter in turn the applicant's last name, address and date of birth in the corresponding fields.

The screen could then look like Figure 5.3, for example.

TIP INSERT OR OVERWRITE?

Remember this? You can tell by the display 'INS' or 'OVW' in the status bar whether your inputs are being inserted or are overwriting the existing entry. You can also see that the cursor is represented differently depending on whether Insert or Overwrite is set. You will learn more about this in Chapter 17.

You can switch between Insert and Overwrite at any time, simply by clicking on the display in the status bar.

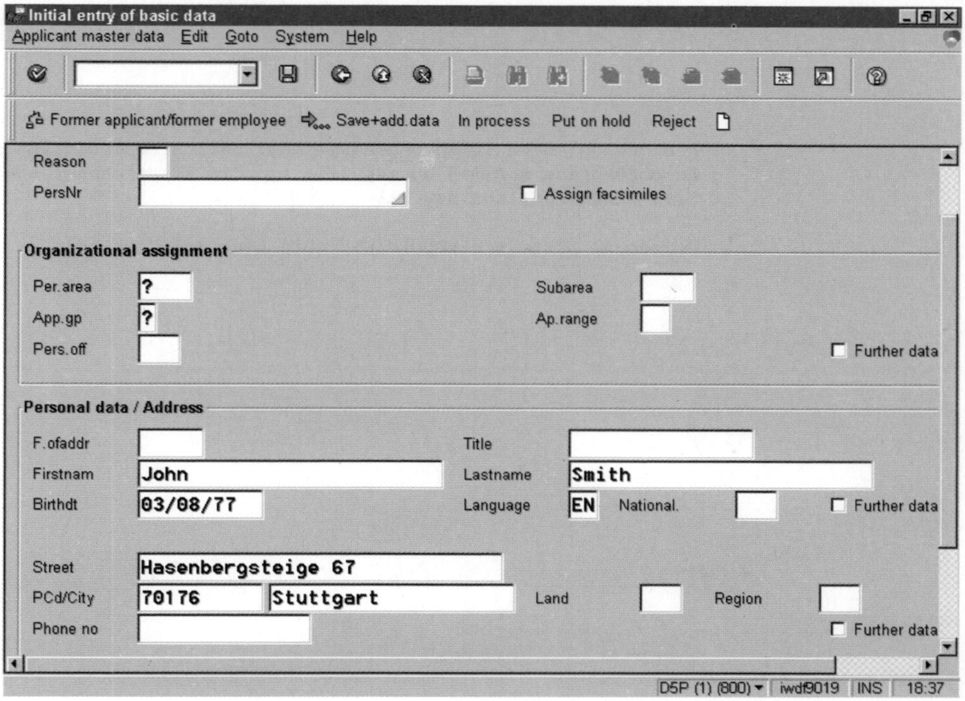

FIGURE 5.3 Example of data for an applicant

DISPLAYING HELP FOR FIELDS

You should not have had any trouble at all in entering the data so far. It's easy to see which fields are intended to accept the first and last name and date of birth respectively.

In some cases, though, the field names are shortened. It may be that you are not sure what the abbreviation means, or which data should be entered in this field.

You can get assistance on this: you can obtain help on any field. This is how:

How to display the help text for a field

1 Click in the field for which you want to call Help, e.g. in the 'Per.area' field.

2 Press the key (F1), or click in the standard toolbar on the symbol ⑦ (FIELD HELP).

The help for this field is displayed (Figure 5.4). Since it can be called with the (F1) key, field help is also known as F1 help.

⌐ Help - Initial entry of basic data ▣   ☒

Personnel area

A personnel area is an organizational entity representing an area within an enterprise defined by specific aspects of personnel administration, time management and payroll.

Personnel areas are subdivided into personnel subareas.

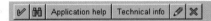

| ✔ | 👓 | Application help | Technical info | ✏ | ✖ |

FIGURE 5.4   F1 help for the Per.area field

TIP   DOES F1 HELP LOOK DIFFERENT FOR YOU?

If F1 help is displayed differently for you, this is because of a particular setting. You can pick out the setting that appeals to you. The next section tells you how to make this setting.

3   Click on ✔ or press (Return) to close help again.

4   Display the help for a few other fields.

You will be amazed at how much information you can find in this way. But that is not all you can display with help. You will learn in Chapter 8 about the other possibilities.

5.5   **SPECIFYING SETTINGS FOR F1 HELP**

F1 help can be displayed in two ways: as you have seen in Figure 5.4.

How to change the F1 help presentation

1   Choose HELP | SETTINGS.

A dialog box is displayed (Figure 5.5).

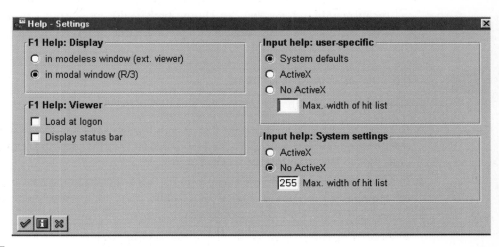

FIGURE 5.5   Settings for F1 help

2   Click on the option 'in modal window (R/3)' (Figure 5.4)

3   Now click on (ENTER)

The setting does not take effect immediately, only when you call the next application.

Radio buttons   In Figure 5.5 you have seen two more field types: radio buttons and checkboxes. (Figure 5.6).

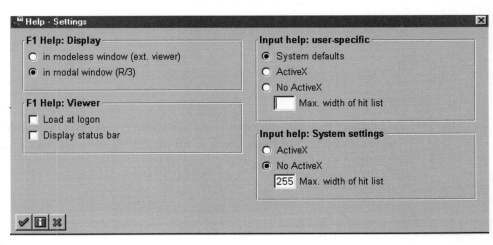

FIGURE 5.6   Checkboxes and radio buttons

The round fields that you just encountered in the previous section are called *Radio buttons*. Such fields are displayed when you have to choose exactly one of several options.

Checkboxes

In Figure 5.6 under 'F1 Help: Viewer' you will see *Checkboxes*. If you previously chose the option 'in modeless window (ext. viewer)', you can specify more details for this display type here. You can choose both fields, one only, or none at all. In other words, with checkboxes you can choose one, none or several of the given options.

TIP | **AND IF YOU ARE USING THE KEYBOARD**

Radio buttons and checkboxes can also be selected via the keyboard.

■ To select a radio button, move the cursor with the tab key (Tab) to the relevant group of radio buttons. Then select the required radio button with the (Arrow r) or (Arrow l) key, and press the tab key again to advance the cursor.

■ To select a checkbox, move the cursor with the tab key (Tab) to the relevant field and press the spacebar. If you want to remove the selection, press the spacebar once more.

How to specify settings for display in the external viewer

1 If you have selected the field 'in modeless window (ext. viewer)', you can make further settings. To do so, choose HELP | SETTINGS once more.

2 Before F1 help is displayed, it must be loaded. That can take a little while. You can specify that F1 help should already be loaded during logon. It is then displayed faster the first time it is called.

3 You can specify that the window in which the help is displayed should have a status bar. Click on the field 'Display status bar'. This shows information similar to that in the main window status bar.

We will study the remaining settings in Chapter 8.

5.6 | **CHECK INPUT**

The data you have just input is not yet saved. If you close the window now, the data is lost. However, the data cannot be saved until all essential entries are made.

5.6.1   Mandatory Field

A field that must always be filled in is also called a *Required entry field*. You recognize such a field by the fact that it contains a question mark until you enter a value. However, there are exceptions. Not all required entry fields are flagged in this way: sometimes an entry in a field only becomes essential if a certain other field is filled in. But don't worry – you will soon find out which fields still require input: SAP R/3 gives corresponding messages in the status bar.

How to check the entered data

▨ Press (Enter).

If not all required entry fields are filled, you will receive a message about this in the status bar. This message points out which fields still need entries.

Our example still lacks some details, as you can see from the question marks in the fields 'Per.area' (Personnel area) and 'App.gp' (Applicant group).

To enter the necessary details in these fields, you must know a valid personnel area, and also know the existing applicant groups. SAP R/3 provides input help, which will be presented in the next chapter, to assist you with this.

CHAPTER 6

Input values: How to find the values you want

In the last chapter you saw that there is a predefined value range for some fields. For example, for the personnel area, you can only input an area that is defined for your company.

Luckily, you do not need to know the possible values for a field by heart: you can display or search for the possible input values.

6.1 DISPLAYING POSSIBLE VALUES – THE VALUE HELP

Value help

Value help shows which values are allowed for a field. You can simply choose the appropriate value from a list. Another advantage here is that you cannot mistype anything when entering the value.

TIP | **FOR WHICH FIELDS IS THERE VALUE HELP?**

You can tell when you put the cursor in a field whether there is value help on it: If the symbol ⬇ is displayed beside the field, there is a value list for it.

We can now continue with the example from the previous chapter – initial entry of applicant data – and fill in the remaining fields.

How to choose a value from a value list

1 Resume the example from Chapter 5, or choose the menu function HUMAN RESOURCES | PERSONNEL MANAGEMENT | RECRUITMENT once more in the SAP R/3 start window (cf. Figure 2.3).

The INITIAL ENTRY OF BASIC DATA window is displayed (Figure 6.1).

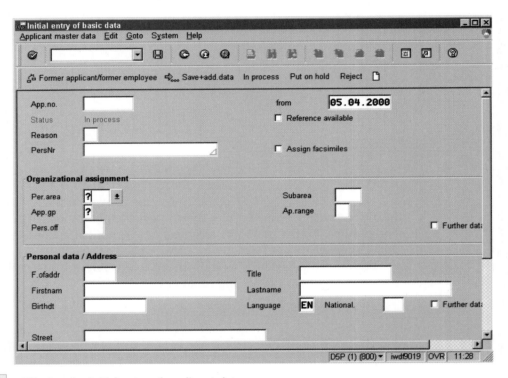

FIGURE 6.1 Window for initial entry of applicant data

The cursor is in the field 'Per.area', and to the right of the field you can see the symbol for the value help.

2 Click on the value help symbol, or press (F4).

The value list with the permissible personnel areas is displayed (Figure 6.2).

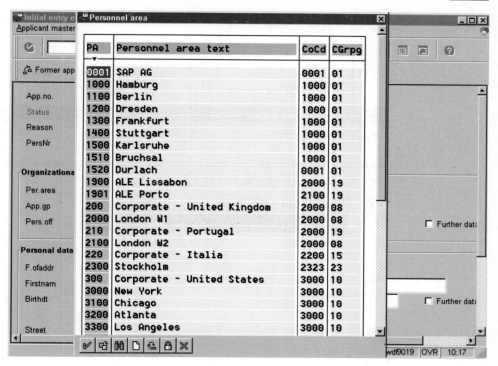

PA	Personnel area text	CoCd	CGrpg
0001	SAP AG	0001	01
1000	Hamburg	1000	01
1100	Berlin	1000	01
1200	Dresden	1000	01
1300	Frankfurt	1000	01
1400	Stuttgart	1000	01
1500	Karlsruhe	1000	01
1510	Bruchsal	1000	01
1520	Durlach	0001	01
1900	ALE Lissabon	2000	19
1901	ALE Porto	2100	19
200	Corporate - United Kingdom	2000	08
2000	London W1	2000	08
210	Corporate - Portugal	2000	19
2100	London W2	2000	08
220	Corporate - Italia	2200	15
2300	Stockholm	2323	23
300	Corporate - United States	3000	10
3000	New York	3000	10
3100	Chicago	3000	10
3200	Atlanta	3000	10
3300	Los Angeles	3000	10

FIGURE 6.2   Possible values for the personnel area

TIP   **DOES THE VALUE HELP LOOK DIFFERENT FOR YOU?**

As in the case of the F1 help, you can also specify the type of presentation for the value help. This may cause the illustrations that follow to look rather different for you. Do not let this confuse you; the procedure is much the same. You will find out in the next section how to make this setting.

3   Double-click on the required entry, or select the entry by setting the cursor on it, and then press (Return).

The value list is closed, and the chosen value is transferred to the INITIAL ENTRY OF BASIC DATA window.

You can also specify a different display form for the value help. See the example in Figure 6.3. You can change the presentation at any time.

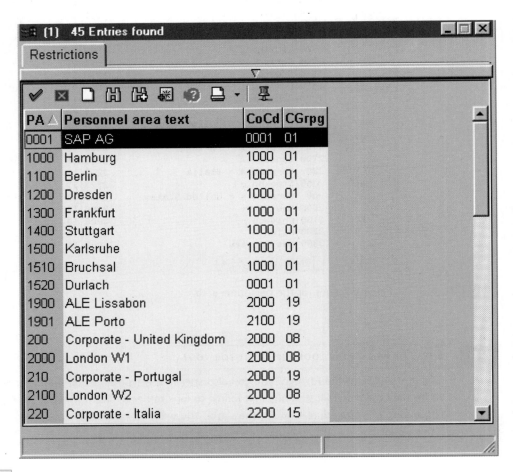

PA △	Personnel area text	CoCd	CGrpg
0001	SAP AG	0001	01
1000	Hamburg	1000	01
1100	Berlin	1000	01
1200	Dresden	1000	01
1300	Frankfurt	1000	01
1400	Stuttgart	1000	01
1500	Karlsruhe	1000	01
1510	Bruchsal	1000	01
1520	Durlach	0001	01
1900	ALE Lissabon	2000	19
1901	ALE Porto	2100	19
200	Corporate - United Kingdom	2000	08
2000	London W1	2000	08
210	Corporate - Portugal	2000	19
2100	London W2	2000	08
220	Corporate - Italia	2200	15

FIGURE 6.3   Value help – a different presentation

How to set the value help display

1   Choose HELP | SETTINGS.

The familiar dialog box, also used for setting F1 help, is displayed (Figure 6.4).

2   If you want the value help to be displayed with tab pages as in Figure 6.3, mark the field 'ActiveX' under 'Input help: user-specific'.

Help - Settings

F1 Help: Display
- ○ in modeless window (ext. viewer)
- ◉ in modal window (R/3)

F1 Help: Viewer
- ☐ Load at logon
- ☐ Display status bar

Input help: user-specific
- ◉ System defaults
- ○ ActiveX
- ○ No ActiveX
  - ☐ Max. width of hit list

Input help: System settings
- ○ ActiveX
- ◉ No ActiveX
  - 255 Max. width of hit list

FIGURE 6.4   Settings for F1 and value help

The setting becomes effective when the next application is called.

6.3   **MAKING IT FASTER STILL**

If you are looking for a particular value, you do not have to scroll through the entire list until you see what you want. SAP R/3 offers you several options for finding the required value faster. Choose the best method according to the situation:

Sort

- For example, if you know the initial letter of the value, you can sort the list alphabetically, thus making it quicker to find the value you want.

Restrict value range

- If you won't be considering all the displayed values, but only those meeting certain criteria, you can restrict the value range. This shortens the list to the values that satisfy the given criteria.

Find value

- If you want to find out whether a particular value is included in the list, enter the value and let SAP R/3 search for it.

The precise method is described in the next sections. The starting point remains the INITIAL ENTRY OF BASIC DATA window (cf. Figure 6.1).

How to sort a value list

1   Display the value list for the 'Per.area' field once more.

2   Click on the title of the column on which you want to sort the value list, e.g. the column 'Personnel area text'.

The value list is sorted on the personnel area text. It is in ascending order, i.e. the list begins with the letters closest to the beginning of the alphabet.

3   If you want to sort the value list in descending order, click again on the column title.

TIP   **WHICH COLUMN DETERMINED THE SORT ORDER?**

You can tell which column the entries are sorted on by a small triangle beside the name of the relevant column. Figure 6.6 shows you an example.

How to restrict the value range

1   Display the value list for 'Per.area' again (cf. Figure 6.2).

2   Click on the symbol ▣ (RESTRICT VALUE RANGE) in the standard toolbar at the lower end of the value list, or press (Shift) + (F5).

A dialog box appears in which you can specify selection criteria for the values to be displayed (Figure 6.5).

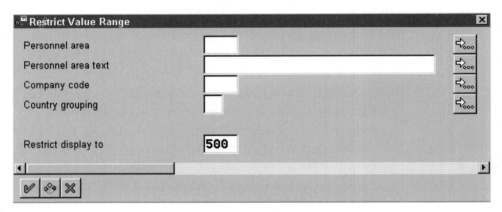

| **FIGURE 6.5** | Restrict value range |

3   For example, you can stipulate that only the personnel areas belonging to a particular company code should be displayed. Do this by entering the company code you want, e.g. '1000', in the 'Company code' field.

The value list is reconstructed, and now only contains the personnel areas for company code '1000' (Figure 6.6).

As you can see, the value list has its own standard toolbar, with which you can process the list. If necessary you can restrict the value range still more.

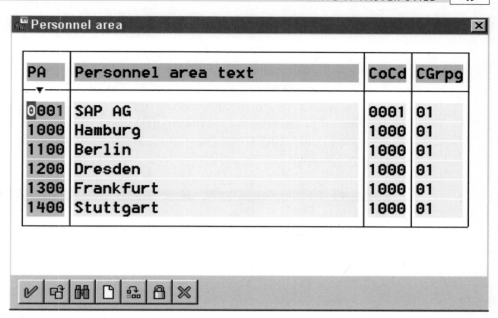

FIGURE 6.6   Restricted value range

How to search for a particular value

1   Display the value list for 'Per.area'.

2   Click in the standard toolbar at the lower end of the value list on the symbol (FIND), or press (Ctrl) + (F).

   The search window shown in Figure 6.7 appears.

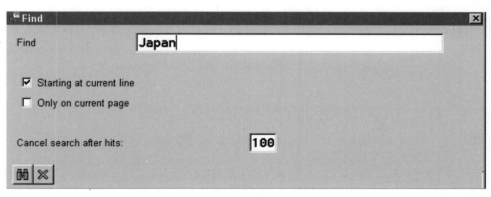

FIGURE 6.7   Search for the personnel area 'Japan'

3   Now enter the personnel area for the search, in our example 'Japan'.

If the value is not included in the list, you receive a message to this effect. If the value was found, a hit list is output as in Figure 6.8.

4   Mark the entry you want, and click on POSITION CURSOR.

The window is closed, and you see the complete value list again. The list is scrolled to the point where the required value appears. You can now choose it with a double click. The value is then transferred to the INITIAL ENTRY OF BASIC DATA window.

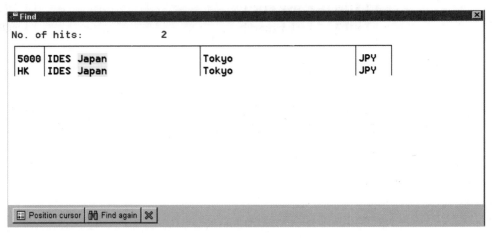

FIGURE 6.8   Hit list. The search term is marked

You now know about value lists. They are very handy in many cases. However, if there are a lot of possible values for a field, it is no longer convenient to show them all in a value list. In such cases SAP R/3 provides search helps. They will be introduced in the next section.

To enable you to follow the examples of the next chapter on your computer, you should now cancel the 'Initial data entry' application.

How to cancel the application

■ Click in the standard toolbar on ✖ (CANCEL).

The application is cancelled without your data being checked or saved. The RECRUITMENT window is displayed again, and you are ready to start on the examples described in the next section.

6.4   SEARCHING SELECTIVELY FOR VALUES – SEARCH HELPS

Search help

If you are looking for a particular person's personnel number, for instance, you can find it by using the person's name. You simply enter the name, and SAP R/3 finds the associated personnel number for you. Such search helps are also called *matchcodes*.

> **TIP**   **WHICH FIELDS HAVE ASSOCIATED SEARCH HELPS?**
>
> A field in which you can use search helps to find values is normally recognizable by a small tri-angle in the upper right corner. But there are exceptions even to this rule. If you are not sure, put the cursor in the field, and press (F4). You will get either a search window or value help, or a message that no search help is available.

Example

Suppose now that you have received an application from the employee John Miller, who is applying internally for another job. Once again your task is the initial entry of applicant data. Since Miller is an employee of your firm, his details are already recorded. SAP R/3 offers the following support so that you do not have to enter the data a second time: you need only enter the employee's personnel number, and SAP R/3 displays the applicant's details in the INITIAL ENTRY OF BASIC DATA window. So now you need to find Miller's personnel number.

How to use search helps

1   Open the INITIAL ENTRY OF BASIC DATA window again, by choosing the menu function HUMAN RESOURCES | PERSONNEL MANAGEMENT | RECRUITMENT in the SAP R/3 start window (cf. Figure 2.3).

2   Set the cursor in the 'PersNr' field, and press (F4).

A dialog box is displayed for searching for the personnel number. Several search helps are available for the personnel number. Since we want to search using the name in this example, we need the search help LAST NAME – FIRST NAME. You can see this in Figure 6.9.

> **TIP**   **IS A DIFFERENT SEARCH HELP DISPLAYED?**
>
> If a different search help is displayed initially, begin by choosing the appropriate search help.
> If value help is displayed as in Figure 6.2, click on 🔲 (CHOOSE SEARCH HELP). The window SEARCH HELP SELECTION (cf. Figure 6.10) is displayed. Choose 'Last name – First name', and press (Return).
> If the value help is displayed as in Figure 6.3, simply click on the tab page LAST NAME – FIRST NAME.

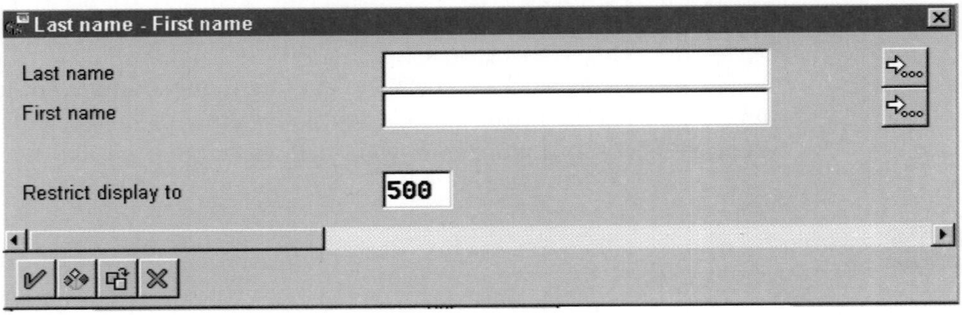

FIGURE 6.9 Searching for the personnel number using the name

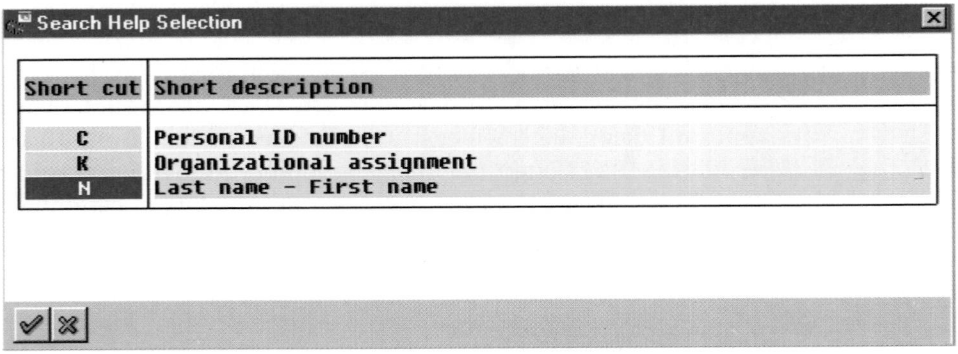

FIGURE 6.10 These search helps are available for the personnel number

3 Now enter 'John' and 'Miller' in the relevant fields in the LAST NAME – FIRST NAME window (see Figure 6.9), and press (Return).

4 If the entry 'John Miller' was found, a hit list is displayed, and you can choose an entry from it. John Miller's personnel number is then transferred to the INITIAL ENTRY OF BASIC DATA window.

TIP IS THE HIT LIST EMPTY?

If the hit list is empty, look for an employee name that is held in the system. For instance, you can display all employees whose last names begin with 'M'. Do this by entering 'M*' for last name in the LAST NAME – FIRST NAME window. The asterisk stands for any number of characters. After you press (Return), you get a hit list of all employees whose last name begins with 'M'. Choose a name.

5 Now indicate in the INITIAL ENTRY OF BASIC DATA window that this is an internal application. Do this by displaying the value help for the field 'App.gp' and choosing the appropriate entry, in our case '2'.

6 You still have to specify whether it is an unsolicited application, or an application in response to a job advertisement. Let's suppose it is an unsolicited application. So display the value help for the field 'SpApGrp', in 'Further data',and choose an entry.

7 Press (Return).

And you did it – John Miller's details are displayed, and you saved yourself a lot of typing (Figure 6.11).

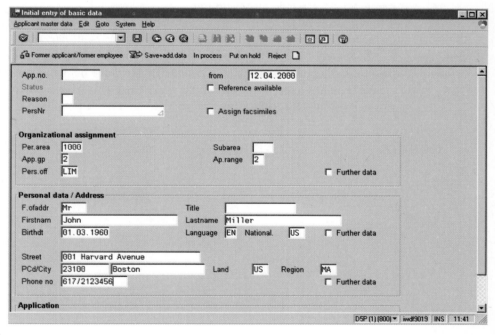

FIGURE 6.11 Completed form

TIP MILLER OR MILLAR?

You are not sure how to spell a name? In the search, simply replace the doubtful character with a placeholder, e.g. Mill*r. A search with 'Mill*r' could return the search result shown in Figure 6.12.

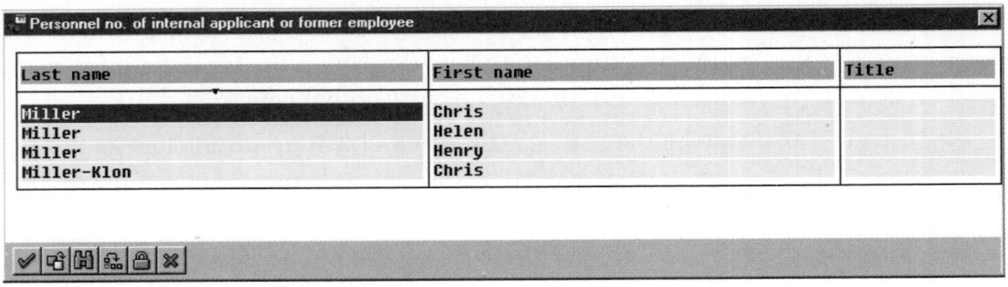

FIGURE 6.12 Result of search for Mill*r

Placeholder for several characters

Remember that the asterisk can stand for several characters. So, for instance, the name 'Milliner' would also be found.

Placeholder for one character

If you want to avoid that, use + as a placeholder. The plus sign replaces exactly one character. If you were searching as above for 'Mill+r', 'Milliner' would not be found.

What next?

You already have the tool for entering data in a form: You can set the cursor in the field of your choice, input data in a field, display value help and use search helps.

In the next chapter you can apply everything you have learned so far and work through a complete application – as you will later do in practice.

CHAPTER 7

Applications: A few examples

You have already seen how to fill in the fields of an application. Now we want to work all the way through a few applications.

7.1 THE FIRST EXAMPLE

Let's stay with the application you already know for the time being: the initial entry of applicant data. Let's assume you want to enter Mr Kirby's data. He is not employed in your company. So, unlike the example in the previous chapter, this involves an external application.

An application can have any number of fields. However, you do not always have to fill them all in.

TIP | WHICH FIELDS MUST BE FILLED IN?

If you do not know which fields you must fill in, you can press (Return). SAP R/3 then checks your inputs. If there are still unfilled required fields, you will receive a message to this effect. This lets you see which details are still needed. However, checking and processing your data naturally takes a little while and puts pressure on the network. So it is faster if you make a note of which fields have to be completed, or check up beforehand in the help. You will learn more about help in Chapter 8.

How to use messages

1   Display the INITIAL ENTRY OF BASIC DATA window again (Figure 7.1).

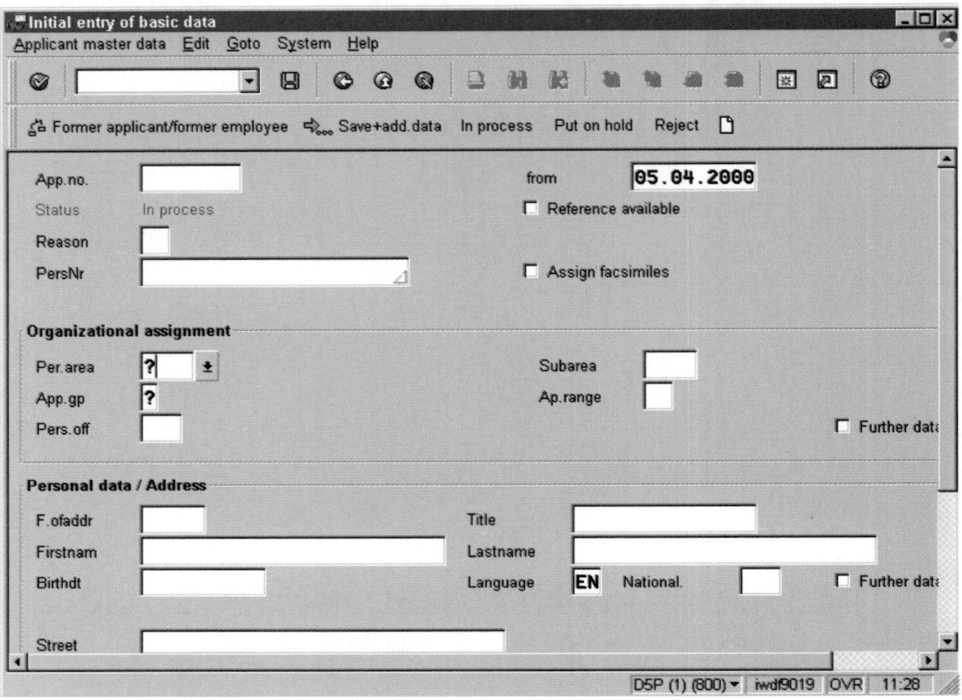

FIGURE 7.1   Window: INITIAL ENTRY OF BASIC DATA

2   The cursor is in the field 'Per.area'. Choose a personnel area, e.g. '1000'.

3   Required entry fields, which are identified by a question mark, must always be filled in. In our example, the field 'App.gp' is a required entry field. Indicate that this is an external applicant. In our example you do so by choosing the value '1'.

4   If you do not know now which fields still must be completed, press (Return).

You will see from the status bar that an entry is still missing, and the cursor is set in the field 'Ap.range'.

5   Enter e.g. '2' as the applicant range, and press (Return) again.

A message in the status bar now points out that you have to enter the applicant's last name (Figure 7.2). This is used, for example, to check whether the

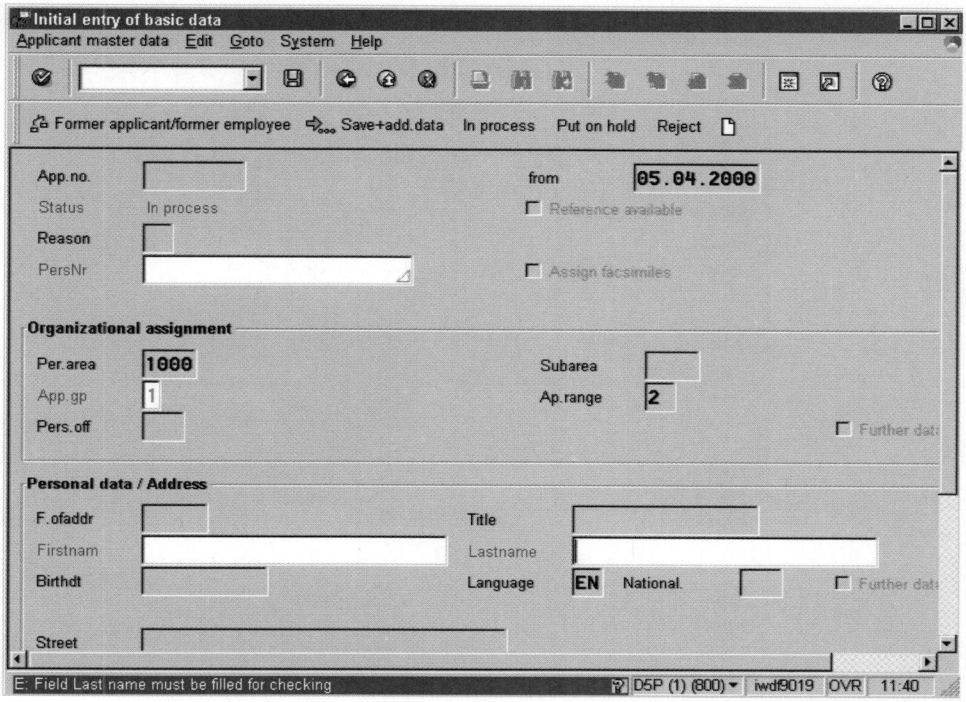

FIGURE 7.2   Last name is still missing

applicant was previously employed in your company, or has applied more than once. In this case the applicant's details would automatically be displayed for you, and you would not need to input them.

6   So the next input has to be in 'Last name'. Enter 'Kirby'.

7   Choose the entry 'Mr' at the same time in the 'Form of address' field, and press (Return) again.

SAP R/3 reports in the status bar that you must specify whether it is an unsolicited application, or an application in response to a job advertisement.

8   In our example we are assuming an unsolicited application. So choose a value from the value list for the field 'SpApGrp', in 'Further data' and press (Return) again.

Your screen should now look like Figure 7.3.

SAP R/3 has completed the field 'Pers.off' automatically. No further details are requested. You can now save your inputs.

Save   **9**   Click in the standard toolbar on 🖫 (SAVE), to save your data.

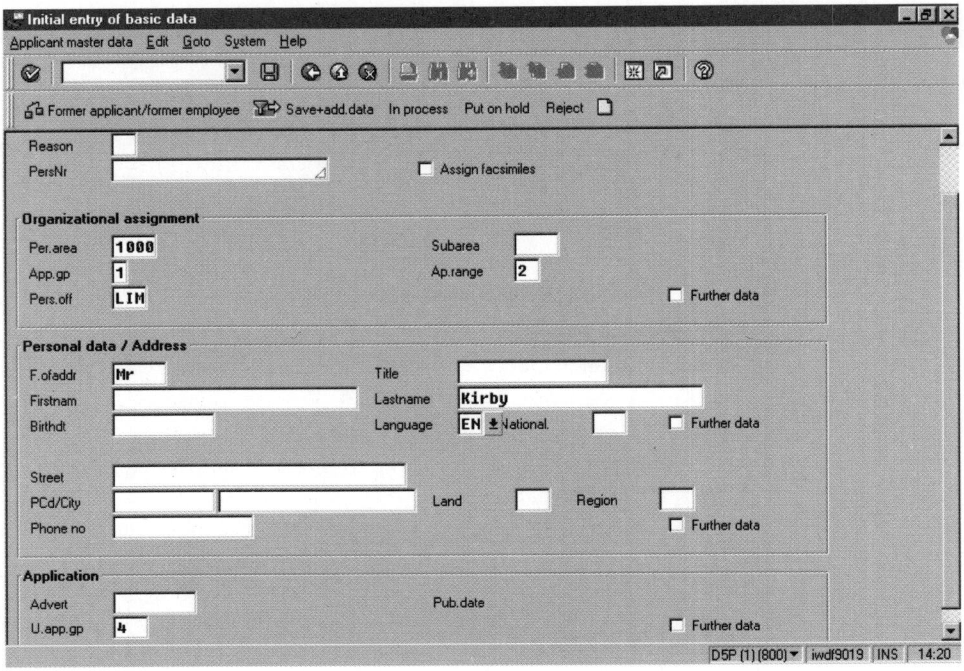

FIGURE 7.3   No further messages in the status bar

Your data is now temporarily stored, and a continuation window appears containing the data that has already been entered (Figure 7.4).

Since Mr Kirby is unknown in the company in our example, the personal details such as his first name still have to be entered.

10 Fill in the rest of the necessary fields. When no further data is requested, save again by clicking on ⊟.

The data is now finally saved, and you will receive the message you see in Figure 7.5.

As you see, an applicant number has been assigned automatically. We can subsequently find Mr Kirby's data by using this number. There's no need to make a note of the number, though: there are corresponding search helps, as you saw in Chapter 6.

TIP   SPEEDING IT UP

When you are used to an application, you should fill in the necessary fields and only press (Return) afterwards. This saves time, because your data has to be checked less often, and the network load is reduced.

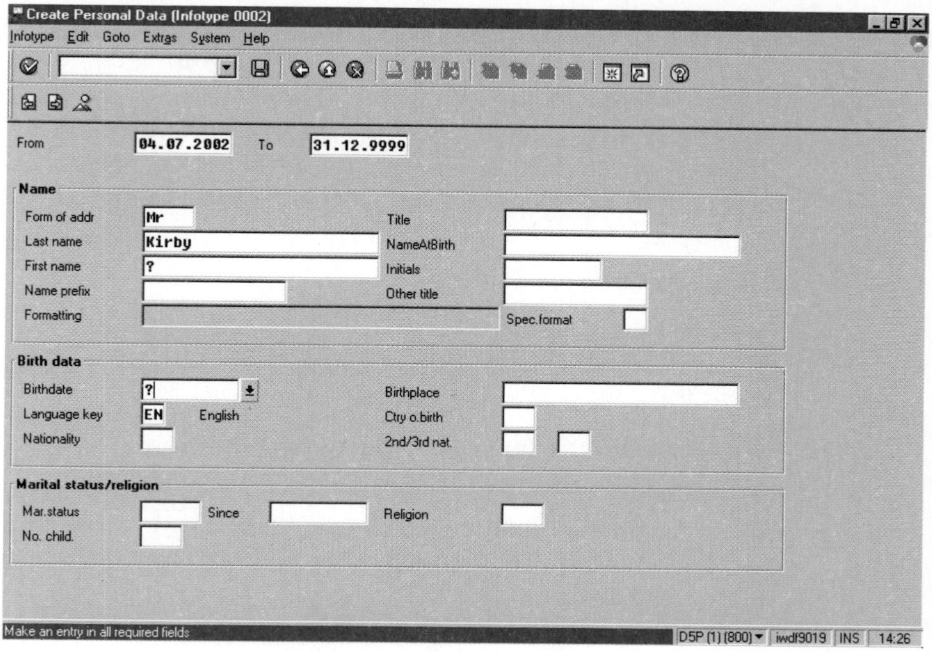

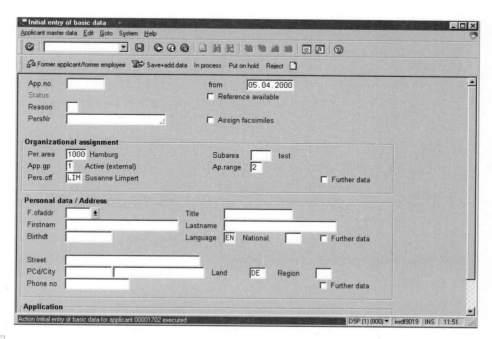

FIGURE 7.4   We continue here after the basic data

FIGURE 7.5   The applicant data has been successfully entered – we can continue

7.2 APPLICATIONS – THE GENERAL FLOW

You have seen an example of how you work with applications. However, the individual steps can differ enormously according to the application area and the application. To make sure you can also find your way around other applications, we will now go through these individual steps in a rather more general form.

How to work with applications

1 Start the required application.

2 Fill in the required entry fields indicated by a question mark, and the other necessary fields.

3 After filling in all necessary fields, press (Return).

4 Further windows may be displayed. Fill these in too.

5 When all the data has been entered, click on 💾 (SAVE). To prevent any accidental loss of data, you will be prompted to save it if you quit the window without doing so.

7.3 FINDING AND EDITING DATA

Suppose now that an applicant has been hired for your company. So far you have only entered the essentials. Now you need to record more data, e.g. bank details. How do you go about this? First you have to find the previously entered data. Then you can supplement it. This is a very common procedure in SAP R/3, and you will come across it frequently in other modules and application areas.

How to find data

1 Display the RECRUITMENT window again (cf. Figure 4.4). If you did the example in this chapter, click on ⬆ until you see the window again. Otherwise log on, and choose HUMAN RESOURCES | PERSONNEL MANAGEMENT | RECRUITMENT from the menu bar in the SAP R/3 start window.

2 Click in the button bar on MAINTAIN APPLICANT MASTER DATA.

The window MAINTAIN APPLICANT MASTER DATA is displayed (Figure 7.6).

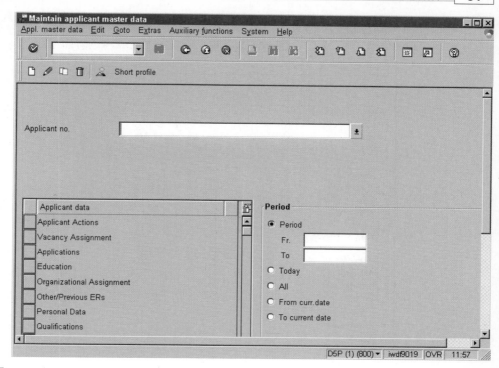

FIGURE 7.6   The initial window for maintaining the applicant master data

Initial window

In this window, you first choose the applicant you want, then you specify which data you want to enter or change. You will often come across such windows in SAP R/3. They are referred to as *Initial windows* or initial screens.

Reference number

To choose the applicant, you can input into the 'Applicant no.' field the number that was automatically assigned during entry of the basic data – if you know the number. Such numbers are also referred to as *Reference numbers*. Don't know the reference number? No problem – you can find it by searching with the applicant's name. Does this process seem familiar? Correct – this is a search help, which you have already seen in Chapter 6.

3   Use the name to find the applicant number. Do this with the search help for the field 'Applicant no.'. In our example it is Mr James Gray.

4   Press (Return).

Some of the applicant data is now displayed (Figure 7.7). The list in the lower half of the window marks the information types that are already entered.

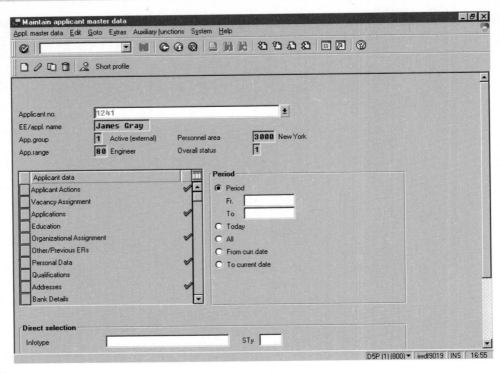

FIGURE 7.7 This data is already entered

5 Click on the button beside the entry 'Bank Details'.

A small triangle is displayed on the button. You know from this that the information type is chosen for editing.

6 Click in the button bar on ⬜ (CREATE) (Figure 7.8).

The CREATE BANK DETAILS window is displayed (Figure 7.9).

7 When your input is completed, click on 💾 (SAVE).

TIP **BACK OR EXIT?**

The 'Create bank details' window gives you a chance to think about the difference between ⬅ (BACK) and ⬆ (EXIT). BACK brings you to the application's initial window (cf. Figure 7.6). EXIT terminates the application, and you return to the RECRUITMENT window (cf. Figure 4.4).

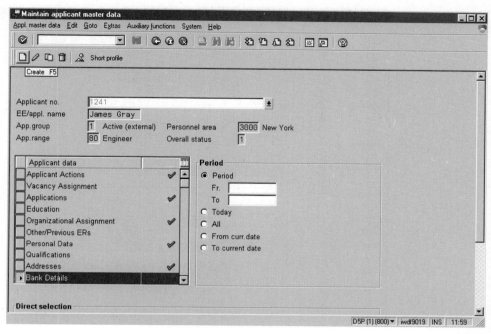

FIGURE 7.8   Choose 'Bank Details' and click on 'Create'

Now you have worked through a couple of applications from beginning to end, as you will do in practice. In the next chapter you will find out how you can make use of the SAP R/3 application help in practice.

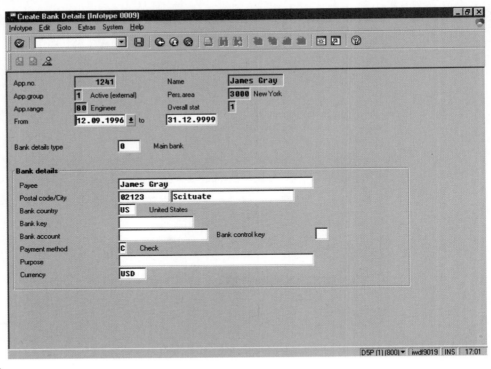

FIGURE 7.9 The bank details are entered here

CHAPTER 8

For those who wish to know more: Help

You have already been introduced to the value help (see Chapter 6) and the field help (see Chapter 5). But SAP R/3 has much more support to offer.

8.1 WHAT DO YOU FIND IN HELP?

SAP R/3 Glossary

The SAP R/3 Glossary is an alphabetically sorted list of terms and their explanations. You will find SAP R/3-specific and general business terms.

Introduction

The introduction describes the elements of the user interface, settings you can make, and basic functions such as logging on and off. This part of the help is of particular interest to beginners. But even after working for a while with R/3, you can still find helpful tips here.

Application help

In contrast to F1 help, application help relates not just to one field, but to the entire application. It includes overview and background information, a description of the functional scope offered by SAP R/3 in the selected area, and tips on how to proceed. Application help is sometimes also called *extended help*.

And the best thing about it is that you don't have to spend a long time searching for the right information: at the touch of a button you can find out precisely what you need to know at the time. That is, you automatically obtain help on the application you are currently using.

SAP Library

The SAP Library contains extensive information on all SAP R/3 modules. As well as help on applications, the SAP Library also contains cross-application help and other useful information.

As you know, SAP R/3 is specially tailored to the needs of your company. The help describes the standard system without adaptations. So it may describe modules and functions that are not in use where you are. Find out whether there are any company manuals or help created especially for the use of SAP R/3 in your company.

8.2 HOW DOES THE HELP LOOK ON YOUR SCREEN? HTML HELP OR STANDARD HTML

SAP R/3 help can be presented in two different ways. You can see the two options in Figures 8.1 and 8.2.

HTML help

HTML help is an HTML format that was developed by Microsoft especially for help presentation. A prerequisite for displaying help in this format is that you work with Windows 95, Windows 98 or Windows NT.

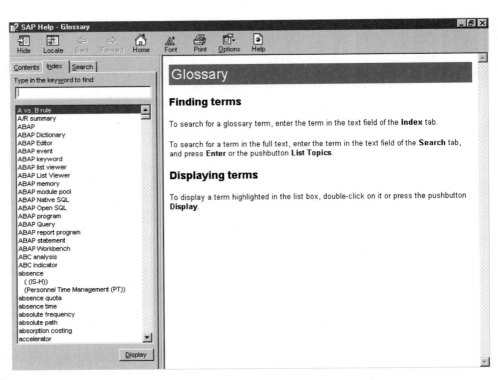

FIGURE 8.1   The glossary as HTML help

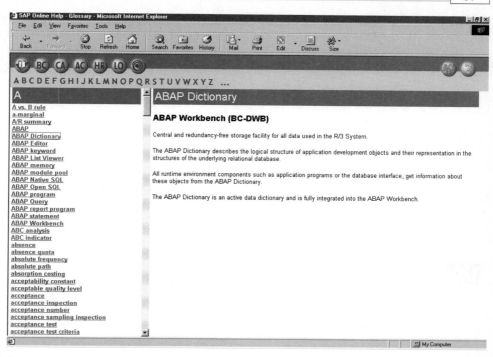

FIGURE 8.2   The glossary in standard HTML format

Standard HTML

Standard HTML format, on the other hand, can be displayed on all computers on which SAP R/3 is installed. Any Web browser can be used to display it.

Help is easy to use in both cases. And the contents are naturally the same.

TIP   **HOW IS THE HELP DISPLAYED ON YOUR SCREEN?**

Give it a try, and see how help is displayed. For example, display the glossary by choosing HELP | GLOSSARY in the menu bar. If the help looks like Figure 8.1, HTML help is in use. In that case read Section 8.3. If the help is displayed as in Figure 8.2, it is standard HTML. In that case, read Section 8.4.

8.3   **HTML HELP**

If your help is displayed as in Figure 8.1, this is where you should be. This section tells you how to make the best use of help.

If you are looking for information on a particular topic, you can find this topic via the table of contents or the keyword directory (index), or with the full text search.

The table of contents and keyword directory are structured as for a book. There is one advantage: you don't have to turn to the relevant page yourself, since it is done automatically.

The full text search provides more than a book can offer: you can search through a complete help component, such as the R/3 Introduction, for every occurrence of a certain term.

How to call help

■ You can call help at any time. You do so by choosing the relevant entry from the HELP menu, either GLOSSARY, INTRODUCTION, APPLICATION HELP or SAP LIBRARY.

TIP   **MORE OPTIONS**

If you have already displayed help on a field, you can also call the application help directly from the F1 help.

How to call application help from F1 help

■ If the F1 help is displayed in 'classic' style, click on APPLICATION HELP to call application help (Figure 8.3).

How to find a topic via the table of contents

1   Select the help component you want from the HELP menu by choosing e.g. HELP | INTRODUCTION (Figure 8.4).

On the first call, the table of contents is normally displayed on the left, as shown in Figure 8.4. If this is not the case, click in the left half of the window on the tab page CONTENTS.

At first you will see only one entry in the table. However, this entry has subentries. You can tell that by the ⊞ in front of the entry.

2   Display the subentries in the table of contents by double-clicking on the displayed entry, or clicking on ⊞ (Figure 8.5).

Help topics are identified by the symbol 📄.

3   Simply click on the help topic of your choice. The text is then displayed in the right half of the window (Figure 8.6).

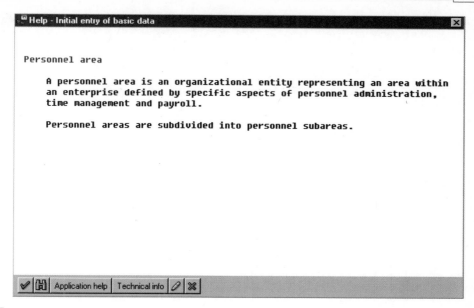

FIGURE 8.3   You can also call application help from F1 help

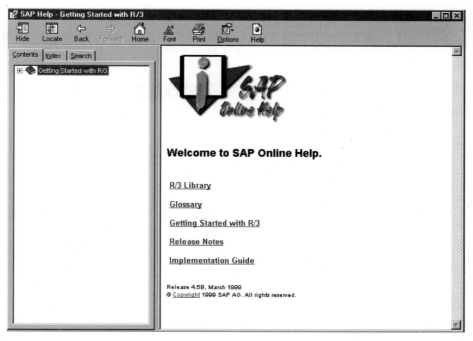

FIGURE 8.4   The introduction

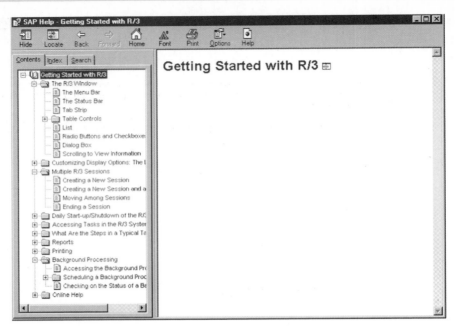

FIGURE 8.5 The next level of the table of contents

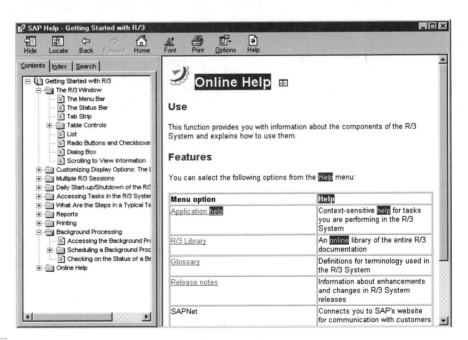

FIGURE 8.6 The introduction contains e.g. 'Help on Help'

How to use the keyword search

1   Display the help, and click in the left half of the window on the tab page INDEX.

An alphabetical list of the keywords is displayed (Figure 8.7).

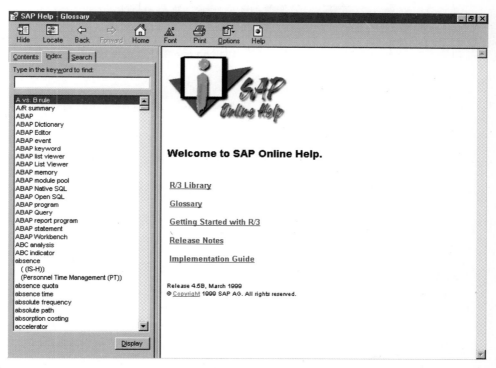

FIGURE 8.7   The keywords can be seen on the left

2   Scroll to the term you are looking for, or enter it in the input field.

3   If this term is shown in the keyword list, you can display the associated text in the right half of the window, by double-clicking on the term. If there are several help topics with this keyword, a selection list appears so that you can make your choice of topic.

How to find a term with the full text search

1   Display the help, and click in the left half of the help window on the tab page SEARCH.

The full text search is displayed (Figure 8.8).

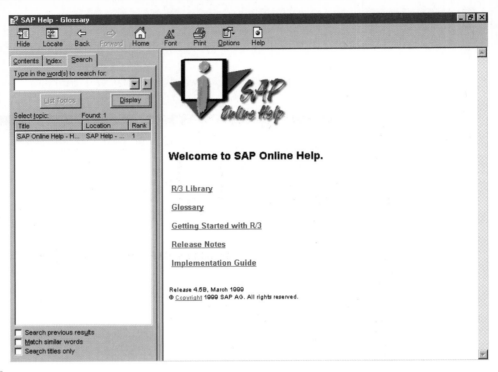

FIGURE 8.8   The term to be found can be entered here

2   Specify the search term in the input field on the left side, and click on LIST TOPICS.

A list of help topics in which the search term occurs is displayed.

3   Choose the help topic you want with a double click.

The help topic is displayed in the right half of the window.

8.4   STANDARD HTML

If your help looks like Figure 8.2, this is the section for you. You will learn here how to call help and find the topic you want.

How to call help

1   You can call help at any time. You do so by choosing the relevant HELP menu option: GLOSSARY, SAP LIBRARY, APPLICATION HELP (Figure 8.9).

The left side of the window shows the contents of the Introduction, the right side shows the chosen help topic.

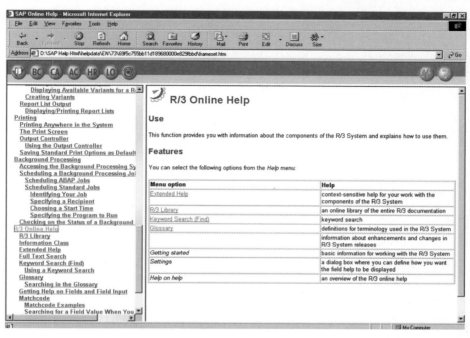

FIGURE 8.9   The help window, using the Introduction as an example

The displayed symbols enable you to switch very easily between the individual help components – a click on the relevant symbol is sufficient. The abbreviations on the symbols stand for the SAP R/3 modules. These symbols get you to the various help components:

- BC – Basis documentation
- CA – Cross-application documentation
- HR – Human resources management
- AC – Accounting
- LO – Logistics

2   Take a little time to browse in help. Click in the left half of the window on a topic that interests you, and read the text displayed for it.

Some help topics include passages underlined in blue. If you click on these texts, you will obtain further information on the topic mentioned in the underlined text.

TIP   **DO YOU WANT TO SEARCH FOR A PARTICULAR TERM?**

Possibly your company uses an add-on product to enable you to search the help for a particular term. If this is the case, you will find the entry FIND in the HELP menu. Give it a try anyway.

CHAPTER 9

For those in a hurry: Calling applications faster

Suppose your company just placed a job advertisement. One application after another lands on your desk, and you are responsible for entering the applicant data. You can call the relevant application through the menus, as you saw in previous chapters. But there are also quicker ways, which are very easy to use in SAP R/3.

9.1 A DOUBLE CLICK IS ENOUGH – SHORTCUTS ON THE WINDOWS DESKTOP

Shortcut

Do you have a computer with Windows 95, Windows 98 or Windows NT? Then you are already familiar with shortcuts. On the Windows desktop, which is displayed after the computer is started, you will see symbols, some of which are linked to programs (Figure 9.1). By double-clicking on a symbol you can start the corresponding program directly, without having to spend time searching for the program in the START menu. Here and in the SAP R/3 user interface, these links are commonly called *shortcuts*. You probably also use a shortcut to log on to SAP R/3.

If you are using Windows 95, Windows 98 or Windows NT, you can make your own shortcuts very easily in SAP R/3. This enables you to start your most frequently used SAP R/3 applications directly from the Windows desktop.

| FIGURE 9.1 | Shortcuts on the Windows desktop |

How to generate a shortcut

1 Start SAP R/3, and log on to the training client.

2 Begin by displaying the window for initial entry of applicant data: Choose HUMAN RESOURCES | PERSONNEL MANAGEMENT | RECRUITMENT, and click on INITIAL ENTRY OF BASIC DATA.

3 Click in the standard toolbar on (GENERATE SHORTCUT).

You will see the dialog box shown in Figure 9.2, in which all the data is already entered.

4 Click on OK.

5 Exit SAP R/3, and log off from SAP R/3.

You will now see your new shortcut on your Windows desktop (Figure 9.3).

You can now call your application quickly with the new shortcut.

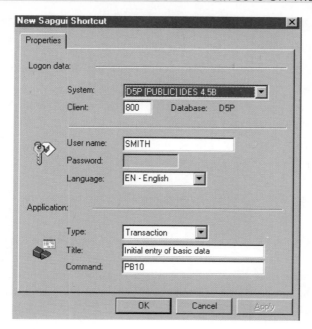

FIGURE 9.2   Generate shortcut

FIGURE 9.3   Your new shortcut

How to go directly into your application

1   Double-click on the shortcut on the Windows desktop.

2   In the displayed dialog box, enter your password in the 'Password' field. Click on LOG ON.

3   When the copyright notice is displayed, click on CONTINUE. You can proceed with your data entry right away!

TIP   **HOW ELSE CAN I USE MY SHORTCUTS?**

Even if you have already started SAP R/3, you can make good use of your shortcuts on the Windows desktop:

■ You can start an application by dragging the shortcut with the mouse into your current SAP R/3 window.

■ Are you already entering data, and want to start a new session? You can simply double-click on the shortcut. The application is started at once in a separate window, without your having to log on again (see Figure 9.4).

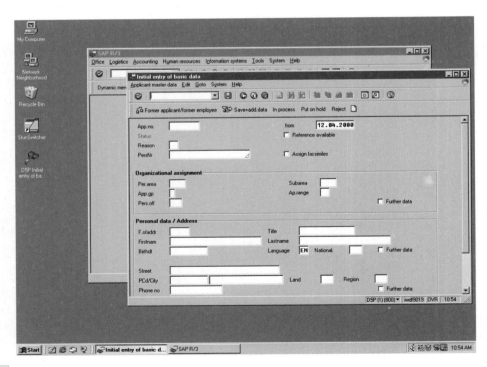

FIGURE 9.4   Start application in a separate window

9.2   SHORT AND SWEET – TRANSACTION CODES

In Chapter 4 you learned how to go to an application through menus. If you work for long with SAP R/3, you might sometimes also find it very handy to branch directly to an application. You can use transaction codes to do this.

Transaction code   A transaction code is a four-character identifier that stands for an application. For example, the transaction code 'PB10' stands for the initial entry of applicant data. Transaction codes allow you to bypass the menus and call an application directly. You do this by entering the transaction code in the command field in the standard toolbar (Figure 9.5).

FIGURE 9.5   Command field in the standard toolbar

Experienced users often know the transaction codes by heart for the applications they use most. This enables them to call the application they want from any window without delay. But remember: it is easy to forget transaction codes. So it is generally better to create shortcuts on the Windows desktop, or collect your frequently used applications in a favourites list. This option will be explained in Chapter 16.

But let's get back to transaction codes. If you do not know the transaction code for an application, it is very easy to find out.

How to find an application's transaction code

1   If you did the last exercise, you should already see the INITIAL ENTRY OF BASIC DATA window. Otherwise you can display it from the SAP R/3 start window, by choosing HUMAN RESOURCES | PERSONNEL MANAGEMENT | RECRUITMENT, and then clicking on INITIAL ENTRY OF BASIC DATA.

2   Click in the status bar on the first of the four fields.

A menu will be displayed, in which you will find the transaction code for the current application (see Figure 9.6).

Now you can try calling an application with its transaction code.

How to use transaction codes

1   First display the SAP R/3 start window again, for example by clicking on ⬅.

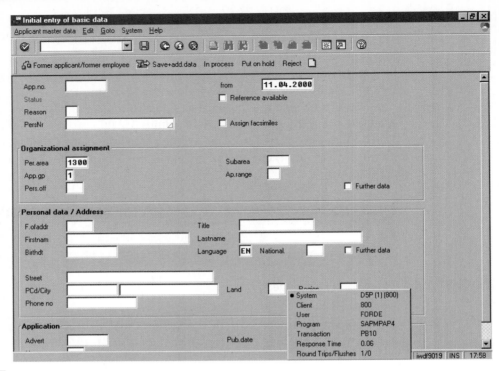

FIGURE 9.6   Finding the transaction code

2   Now we use the command field of the standard toolbar. Enter '/n' followed by the transaction code 'pb10' in the command field.

TIP   **PB10 OR pb10?**

Upper and lower case are not differentiated for transaction codes. So you can use either notation.

The command field should appear as in Figure 9.7.

FIGURE 9.7   Command field with transaction code

3 Press (Return).

You are already at initial entry of applicant data!

TIP | WHY MUST I INPUT '/n'?

In the example, you called the application from the SAP R/3 start window. But you can also call another application when you have already started one. '/n' simply exits your current application and starts the application that you call with the transaction code.

However, you can also start a new session. A new session is a useful option when you want to continue work in your current application and just briefly check on something in another application. Instead of '/n' you then have to enter '/o' (see Figure 9.8).

FIGURE 9.8 | How to start an application in a new session

TIP | WHICH TRANSACTION CODES CAN YOU INPUT?

If you want to know which transaction codes you can input, set the cursor in the command field and press (F1).

One transaction code that you can always input is '/nend'. You can log off with this.

TIP | IF THINGS ARE NOT ADVANCING ...

As with any computer application, it can sometimes happen that the application 'freezes' and nothing advances. If you cannot get any further with ← (BACK) or ⬆ (EXIT), enter '/n' in the command field. Unsaved data will be lost when you do this, but you will be able to continue work afterwards.

In this chapter you learned a few quick ways to get into an application. In the next chapter you will find out how to speed up data input in SAP R/3.

CHAPTER 10

Data input made easy

SAP R/3 offers you numerous options for cutting down on time-consuming and error-prone manual data input. For example, you can put together a personal value list of the values you need most often, or specify that certain fields are always filled with the same data, and so on.

10.1 LESS IS MORE – PERSONAL VALUE LIST

Value lists can sometimes be pretty long, and often you only really need a couple of values. For example, when entering applicant data you can also specify the language. You can select this from a long list. Suppose you are responsible only for English, French and German. All other languages occur only very occasionally. Wouldn't it be nice to have a shortened list, containing only your three most commonly entered languages?

Personal value list

That is easily arranged: you define a personal list, which only contains the entries you often need. If another value is needed, you simply switch to the complete list. This is done as follows.

How to define a personal value list

1 Display the INITIAL ENTRY OF BASIC DATA window again (cf. Figure 4.5).

2 Display the value help for the 'Language' field (Figure 10.1).

3 Mark the first language you want to include in your personal value list, e.g. 'German'.

FIGURE 10.1   Value help for the 'Language' field – very extensive

TIP   SPEEDING IT UP

To find the relevant language faster, you can sort the list alphabetically. Click on the column title 'Long name'.

4   Now click in the standard toolbar on ⬛ (INSERT IN PERSONAL LIST).

The standard toolbar now shows a new symbol. You can use this to display your personal value list ⬛ (PERSONAL VALUE LIST).

5   But first you should add the other two languages. Mark the language you want, and click again on ⬛.

6   Now display your personal value list by clicking on ⬛ (Figure 10.2).

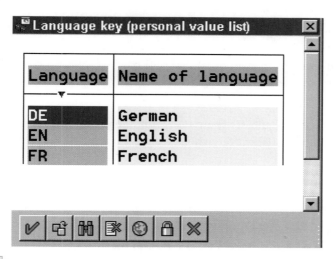

| **FIGURE 10.2** | Your personal value list – easy to view |

7   If you do want the complete list on occasion, just click on 🌐 (ALL VALUES).

8   If you no longer want to keep an entry in your personal value list, choose the entry and click on ⬛ (DELETE FROM PERSONAL VALUE LIST). The entry is only deleted from your personal value list. Of course, it remains as an entry in the list of all values.

| 10.2 | **HOW TO CUT DOWN ON INPUTS – KEEPING OR SETTING DATA** |

Suppose that only people living locally apply for a temporary job. The city in the address is therefore the same for all applicants.

Keeping data

You only need to make this entry once, and then you can simply 'keep it on the screen'. For all the applicants you subsequently enter, the city is then already present. You can still overwrite the entry if necessary.

Setting data

On the other hand, if you are certain that the entry will never be different, you can also 'set' the data. The field in question is then similarly already filled in, but in this case it cannot be overwritten. So, for instance, you can make sure that a particular field is always filled with the same value, and no other value is accidentally entered. Naturally, keeping and setting is not restricted to one field only, but also functions for several fields.

TIP | INPUTTING CODES – THE EASY WAY

Keeping and setting is particularly useful in applications where you have to input numerical codes, such as purchase order numbers, customer numbers etc. It is all too easy to make mistakes when typing these. With keep or set you only have to type and check the entry once, and then it is correct for the next 100 or so.

However, keeping and setting data is not equally appropriate in all modules, so this option is not available everywhere. Just give it a try.

How to keep data on the screen

1   Display the INITIAL ENTRY OF BASIC DATA window again.

Enter e.g. 'New York' in the 'City' field.

2   In the menu bar choose SYSTEM | USER PROFILE | KEEP.

You can now continue working as usual. When you enter the next applicant data, 'New York' is already entered as the city. If necessary, though, you can input a different city.

3   The entry 'New York' is retained until you log off or delete the data you kept. Do this by choosing SYSTEM | USER PROFILE | DELETE in the menu bar.

How to set data

1   Display the INITIAL ENTRY OF BASIC DATA window again.

Enter e.g. 'New York' in the 'City' field.

2   In the menu bar choose SYSTEM | USER PROFILE | SET.

You can now continue working as usual. When you enter the next applicant data, 'New York' is already entered as the city. You can no longer change this entry.

3   The entry 'New York' is retained until you log off or delete the data you kept. Do this by choosing SYSTEM | USER PROFILE | DELETE in the menu bar.

TIP | **TURBOCHARGING**

The (Tab) key always takes you to the next input field. As long as a value is set for a field, it is no longer considered as an input field. Such fields are therefore skipped when you move to the next field with the tab key. So you have significantly speeded up the data input.

In Chapter 15 you will find another way to spare yourself inputs and become even faster.

10.3 COPYING DATA

Does it sometimes happen that you already have data in electronic format, e.g. in an MS Word file or an email, and you would like to input this into SAP R/3? Or conversely, you would like to insert data from SAP R/3 into a different application? You could type the data, but of course it is easier to copy it.

Suppose you are busy entering the applicant data for Ms Shapiro-Montgomery, and want to request missing application documents by email. You want to copy the applicant's name into the email program.

How to copy data

1   In the INITIAL ENTRY OF BASIC DATA window, select the applicant's name by keeping the left mouse button pressed and moving the mouse pointer across the name.

TIP | **AND USING THE KEYBOARD**

Set the cursor at the beginning of the name. Keep (Shift) pressed, and move the cursor to the end of the word by pressing (Arrow r).

2   Then choose 🔲 | CLIPBOARD | COPY in the menu bar, or press (Ctrl) + (C).

3   Set the cursor at the point where you wish to insert the name, and press (Ctrl) + (V). You can also use the application menu function, that of the email program in our example. You will find it in the EDIT menu in most applications.

TIP **AND VICE VERSA**

The other direction – copying from a non-SAP application into a SAP R/3 window field – works in exactly the same way. Naturally, you can also copy within SAP R/3. For example, you can copy the contents of a field into a field in another session. In some applications there are even additional clipboard functions. You will find these under 🔲 | CLIPBOARD.

Copying several fields

So far you have copied the contents of a single field. But SAP R/3 also allows you to copy several fields. This is very useful, especially in tables, as we will see in Section 10.5.

10.4 CUTTING DATA

Instead of copying data, you can also cut it. If you accidentally entered a last name in a field for the first name, for instance, simply cut this name out and then insert it again in the correct field.

Cutting works in much the same way as copying. You can cut data in a non-SAP application and insert it into a SAP R/3 application, or vice versa. And of course you can also cut and insert (paste) data within SAP R/3.

How to cut data

1   Select the data to be cut by marking it and press (Ctrl) + (X) or choose 🔲 | CLIPBOARD | CUT in the menu bar.

2   Place the cursor at the point where you wish to insert the data, and press (Ctrl) + (V). If you are inserting the data in a SAP R/3 window, you can also choose 🔲 | CLIPBOARD | INSERT in the menu bar.

10.5 HOW TO WORK WITH TABLES

In many applications, data is arranged in tables. Imagine a purchase order: for each item in the purchase order, the material group, quantity etc. must be entered. A table is a good solution here: the articles or items are listed in lines, and the various details are entered in columns. A line in such a table is often called a record.

Let's have a look at one of these purchase orders. So we will switch now from the HR department to purchasing. In SAP R/3 that means switching to the Materials management (MM) module.

How to work with tables

1 Display the SAP R/3 start window (cf. Figure 2.3), and choose LOGISTICS | MATE-
RIALS MANAGEMENT | PURCHASING from the menu bar.

The PURCHASING window is displayed.

2 In the menu bar choose PURCHASE ORDER | CREATE | VENDOR UNKNOWN.

The initial window for creating a purchase order is displayed (Figure 10.3).

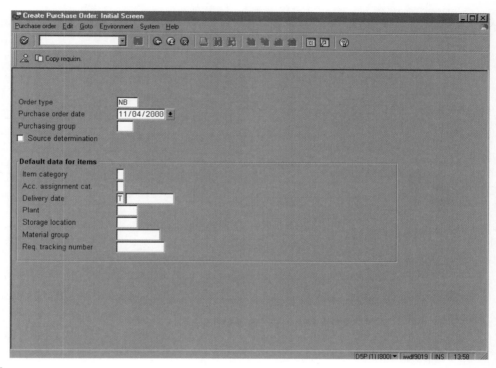

| **FIGURE 10.3** | The initial screen |

Initial window

An initial window of this kind is typical for applications in SAP R/3. You will
come across it in many applications.

3 Choose a value in the 'Purchasing group' field.

Specifying
default data

4 Frequently, some of the details in a purchase order are the same for all items. For
example, if you are mainly ordering goods in a particular material group, you can
enter this right at the beginning. The material group is then entered for every

item. You can overwrite it at any time, though. For example, under 'Default data for items' choose material group 103 for electronics in the 'Material group' field.

5   Now click ✔ (ENTER).

The next window of the application is displayed (Figure 10.4).

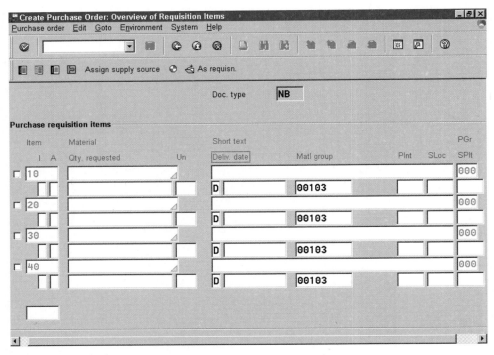

FIGURE 10.4   One presentation option for a table

The window shows the individual purchase order items and the associated details as a table. In the presentation you see in Figure 10.4, two lines are displayed per item. The table titles are also shown as two lines. This compressed display form allows you to see all details for an item without having to scroll to the right.

TIP   **WOULD YOU LIKE TO CHANGE THE PRESENTATION OF THE TABLE?**

Would you rather have just one line displayed per item? No problem – choose EDIT | SWITCH DISPLAY in the menu bar. Now the table looks like Figure 10.5.

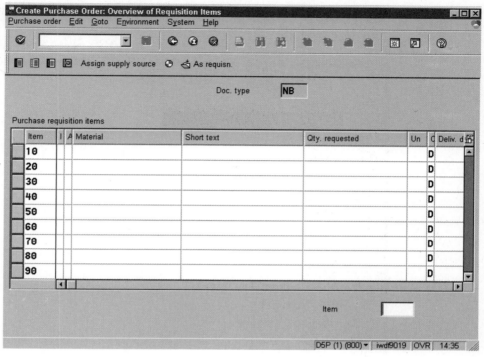

FIGURE 10.5   The table can also be presented in this form

6   Scroll right to find the material group field. You will see that the material group you specified as default value is already entered for every item.

7   Scroll back left, and now choose the item you want to edit, as follows. If you opted for the presentation as in Figure 10.4, select the checkbox to the left of item 10. In a presentation as in Figure 10.5, click on the button to the left of item 10. The record is selected.

8   Now you can fill in its fields. In principle that is done exactly as in the examples that we have already seen. So we do not wish to go into the details of the individual fields here. We would just like to point out a few special features.

Keeping value help on the screen

Table fields often have value help, as covered in Chapter 6. If you have to specify certain values for each item, it is often a good idea to keep the value help on the screen. Then you do not have to call it for every item, and you save yourself a lot of time.

How to keep the value help on the screen

1   Display the value help for the 'Plant' field (Figure 10.6).

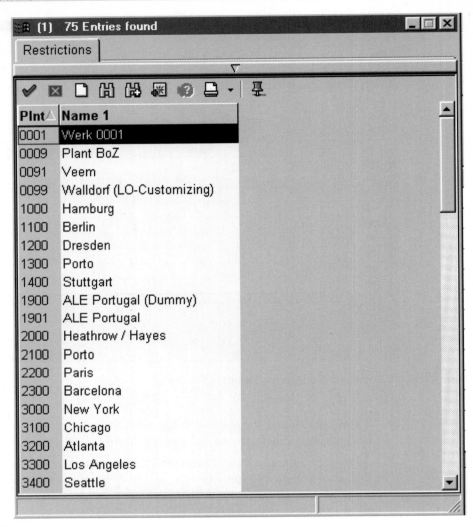

FIGURE 10.6   The value help for the 'Plant' field

2   Click on 🖈 (KEEP VALUES) to keep the value help on the screen.

3   Select a value and click on ✔ (ENTER) to transfer the value into the table.

You can now edit the table just as usual. The value help remains on display, and you won't need to display it again when editing the next item. And of course, you can also put together a personal value list as usual (cf. Chapter 6).

Copying several fields

   Suppose you are ordering 100 pallets each of several materials. For each item you have to enter the value '100' under 'Qty. requested' and the value 'PAL' under 'Un' (Unit). Here too, you can save yourself some typing by copying several fields at once.

How to copy several fields

1   Enter the value '100' under 'Qty. requested' and 'PAL' under 'Un'.

2   Press (Ctrl) + (Y).

The mouse pointer is displayed in crosshair form.

3   Now select the range you want to copy, by moving the mouse pointer over the two fields that you just filled in. The fields are displayed in reverse video, as shown in Figure 10.7.

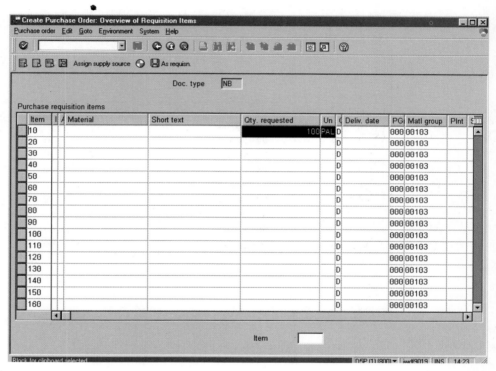

FIGURE 10.7   The marked range can be copied to the clipboard

4   Now press (Ctrl) + (C), to copy the range to the clipboard.

5   Set the cursor in the next line in the 'Qty. requested' column, and press (Ctrl) + (V).

6   The copied range – i.e. the details for the fields 'Qty. requested' and 'Un' (Unit) – is inserted.

This also works with larger ranges than in our example, of course. Think about it when tables have repeated content, and save yourself the input.

TIP **IS THE COLUMN TITLE ABBREVIATED?**

Column titles are often shortened for reasons of space (Figure 10.8). You can see the full form by pointing to the column title with the mouse. The long name is then displayed, as with quick info for symbols. For table columns, this function is also referred to as *Data Tip*.

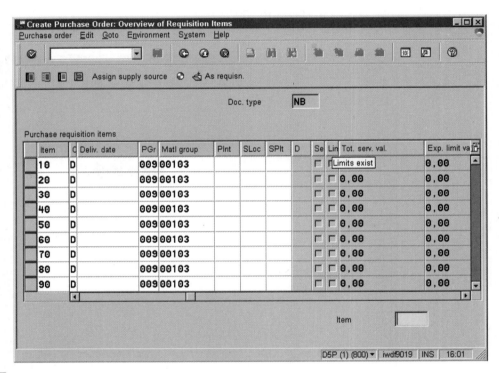

FIGURE 10.8 This is how you see the column title

TIP **WOULD YOU LIKE TO MAKE A COLUMN WIDER?**

To allow tables to display information as clearly as possible on the screen, some columns are made relatively narrow. If you do not like the display, you can change the column widths at any time. Do this by pointing with the mouse at the line bordering the column. The mouse pointer form changes, and you can drag the column to the width you want.

You know quite a lot now about data input. In the next chapter you will learn how to keep track of the stored data with reports.

CHAPTER 11

Keeping track with reports

You work in the HR department, and you would like to know which job applications came in during a certain period? Or who has applied for the recently advertised job? No problem. You can generate a wealth of reports with SAP R/3 that will give you an overview of your data. You can find out with a report what job applications have come in following a job advertisement, for instance.

Report   A report is an ABAP program, which fetches the necessary data from the database. ABAP is the language in which SAP R/3 is largely programmed. When your SAP R/3 system is tailored and enhanced, this is mainly done with new ABAP programs.

To simplify report generation, SAP R/3 contains a whole range of finished ABAP programs, which you only need to call.

11.1   YOUR FIRST REPORT

As a first example, you will generate a report on all job applications that have been received in a particular month.

How to generate a report

1   Start SAP R/3, and log on to the training client.

2   Choose HUMAN RESOURCES | PERSONNEL MANAGEMENT | RECRUITMENT, to display the RECRUITMENT window.

3   In the RECRUITMENT window choose EVALUATIONS | VAR. APPLICANT LIST.

You will see the VARIABLE APPLICANT LIST selection window as shown in Figure 11.1.

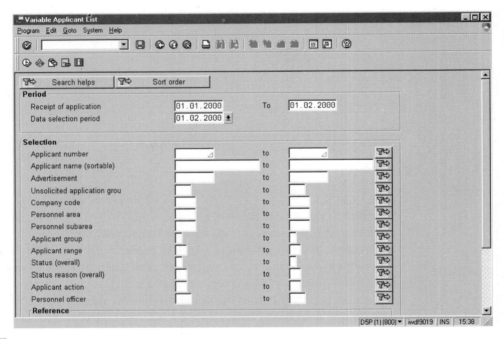

| **FIGURE 11.1** | Selection window: Variable applicant list |

4   In the fields 'Receipt of application' and 'To', enter the period for which you want to display the applicants, e.g. 1 – 25 January 1999. You can also specify a different application period, though. Today's date is already entered as the data selection period, and you can just leave it like that.

5   Pull down the slider box on the right window edge until you can see the lower part of the window. Click on FIELD SELECTION.

A window appears in which you can choose what you want to have displayed. For this example, simply choose 'Applicant number', 'Last name' and 'First name'. The window should look like Figure 11.2.

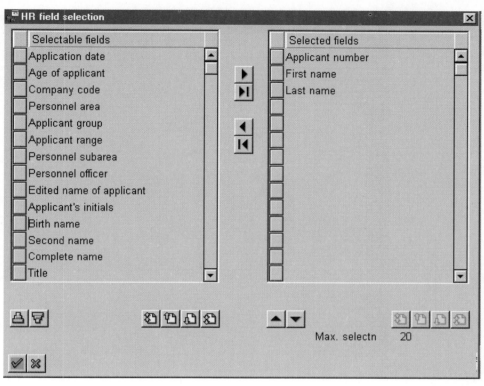

FIGURE 11.2   Choose fields to be displayed

6   Press (Return) to return to the selection window VARIABLE APPLICANT LIST.

7   Start the report generation by clicking on ⏱.

      Your first report is ready! You can see the list of those who applied in the given period (Figure 11.3).

8   Return to the selection window VARIABLE APPLICANT LIST with ⬅ or ⬆.

TIP   **NO REPORT IS DISPLAYED**

SAP R/3 only shows a report if there is any corresponding data. If no job applications were received in the given application period, no report will be generated and you will see the selection window as before. In this case, try it again with a different application period.

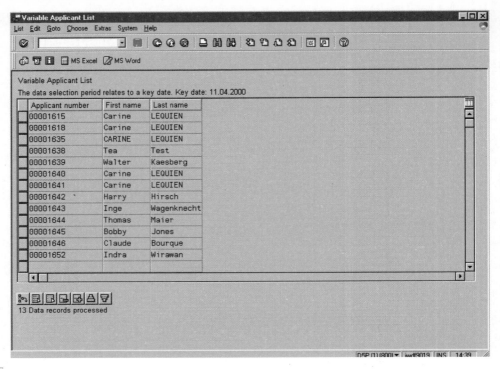

FIGURE 11.3   The first report

11.2   SELECTIVE ACCESS – SPECIFYING SELECTION CRITERIA

Selection criteria

When you generate a report, it should normally display only a subset of the available data. The intention is to gain an overview, not scroll through long lists. Selection criteria enable you to decide how much data your report should contain. You can restrict the report selectively to the data that interests you.

You already set selection criteria in the example in the previous section: you specified a particular application period in the VARIABLE APPLICANT LIST window. The other fields in this window are further selection criteria, with which you can further restrict the applicant data to be displayed.

In the next sections you will learn how to work with selection criteria.

Single value

How to specify a single value

For example, if you want to see all applicants who have applied for a particular job, specify the relevant job advertisement in the selection window.

1   Begin in the VARIABLE APPLICANT LIST selection window. If dates are still entered in 'Receipt of application' and 'To', delete these figures.

2   In the 'Job advertisement' field, choose the job advertisement you want by using value help. If necessary, check again in Chapter 6 about how to use value help.

3   Click on ⊕ to generate the report.

4   Return with ⇐ or ⬆ to the VARIABLE APPLICANT LIST selection window.

Value range

How to specify a value range

As well as single values, you can also specify entire value ranges or intervals as selection criteria. Suppose you would like to display all applicants beginning with the letters A to D. You can achieve this by specifying A and D as the value range.

1   Once again, begin in the VARIABLE APPLICANT LIST selection window. Only today's date in the 'Data selection period' should be entered here. Delete any other selection criteria if present.

2   In the field 'Applicant name (sortable)', enter the letter 'A'.

3   In the field 'to' to the right of the field 'Applicant name (sortable)', enter the letter 'D'. The selection window should look like Figure 11.4.

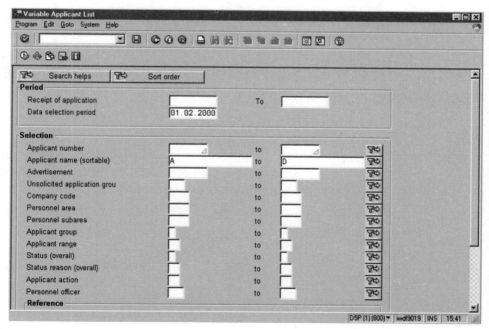

FIGURE 11.4   Give value range

4   Click on 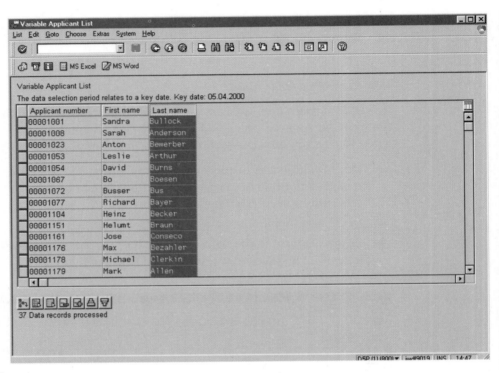 to generate the new report.

5   Check whether in fact only the applicants from A to D are displayed. Sort the applicants by last name for this (see Figure 11.5).

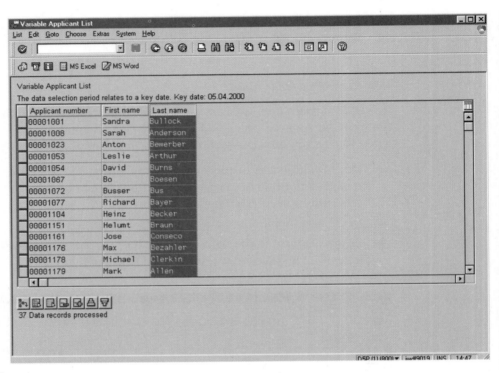

FIGURE 11.5   Sort applicants by last name

6   The list may be so long that you cannot see all the applicants. Click on ⬇ to move a page down, or on ⬇ to scroll right down to the end of the list. If you scroll to the end, you will see that the applicant list only goes to the letter D.

7   Click again on either ⬅ or ⬆ to return to the VARIABLE APPLICANT LIST selection window.

Multiple selection

How to use multiple selection

For some selection criteria, the possibilities in the selection window are insufficient. Suppose you want to display the applicants who are processed in the HR department by Ms May, Ms Short or Ms Miller. For this you need multiple selection.

1   Begin once more in the VARIABLE APPLICANT LIST selection window. Delete the selection criteria apart from today's date in the 'Data selection period' field.

2   Scroll down until you see the field 'Personnel officer'. Scroll to the right, and click on the arrow ⇥… to the right of the 'Personnel officer' field.

The window MULTIPLE SELECTION FOR PERSONNEL OFFICER is displayed (Figure 11.6).

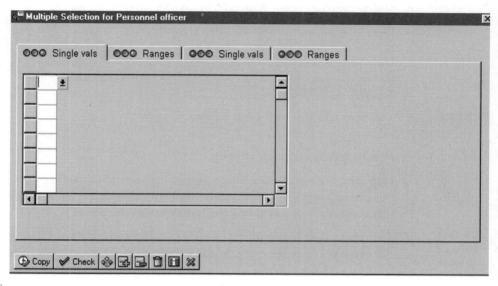

FIGURE 11.6   Tab pages with green lights for multiple selection

3   The tab page SINGLE VALUES with the green light should already be displayed. Otherwise simply click on it.

4   Enter the short name for the first administrator in the first field. The best way is to use value help to look up the abbreviated names.

5   Enter the short names for the other two administrators in the next two fields. Figure 11.7 shows an example of a window with short names entered.

6   Click on COPY to return to the selection window. Do you see how the colour of the arrow ⇥… has changed? You can tell from this that you have specified multiple selection criteria.

7   Click on ⊕ to generate the new report.

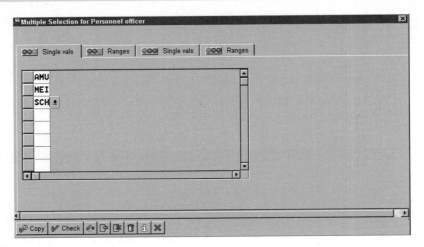

FIGURE 11.7 Multiple selection with single values

Exclusion criteria

How to specify exclusion criteria

Let's take the job applications received in January as a starting point once more. In the new example, all applicants except the trainees are to be displayed. You can do this quite easily by excluding the trainees from the report.

1   Begin once more in the VARIABLE APPLICANT LIST selection window. Delete all selection criteria except today's date in the 'Data selection period' field. Do not forget to delete the selection criteria in the window MULTIPLE SELECTION FOR PERSONNEL OFFICER as well.

2   Click on ⇒... to the right of the field 'Applicant range'.

   The displayed window looks similar to that for multiple selection in the previous example. However, to specify exclusion criteria, you use the tab pages with the red lights (Figure 11.8).

3   Click on the tab page SINGLE VALUES with the red light.

4   The cursor is already positioned in the first field. Display the value help for the field, and choose the trainees from the value help.

5   Click on COPY to return to the selection window. The symbol ▤ to the left of the field 'Applicant range' indicates that this is an exclusion criterion.

6   Click once more on ⊕ to generate the report.

TIP   **HOW CAN I CALL MY REPORT FASTER?**

Just create a shortcut in your Windows desktop! Then all it ever takes to produce your report is a double click. You create a shortcut for a report in exactly the same way as a shortcut for your applications. Look it up in Chapter 9.

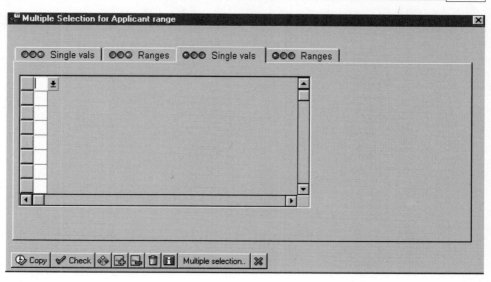

FIGURE 11.8 Specify exclusion criteria

11.3 | MAKING THE MOST OF MULTIPLE SELECTION

In the previous section you used multiple selection to display job applications that are processed by a number of personnel officers. You did this by entering the short names of three administrators into the multiple selection. This procedure is handy for a few entries, but imagine the following situation: You are responsible for purchasing in your company, and you want to know all the finished products that have been ordered. But there are over a hundred different ones in the company. It would take you forever to enter them one by one into the multiple selection. With SAP R/3, though, it is simple to transfer all finished products into the selection in one go. Once again, you can rely on the support of SAP R/3!

How to make the most of multiple selection

1 For this example we will go over to Materials management. Begin in the SAP R/3 start window, and choose LOGISTICS | MATERIALS MANAGEMENT | PURCHASING.

The PURCHASING window is displayed.

2 Choose PURCHASE ORDER | LIST DISPLAYS | BY MATERIAL.

You will see the selection window shown in Figure 11.9.

3 Click to the right of the 'Material' field on ▣.

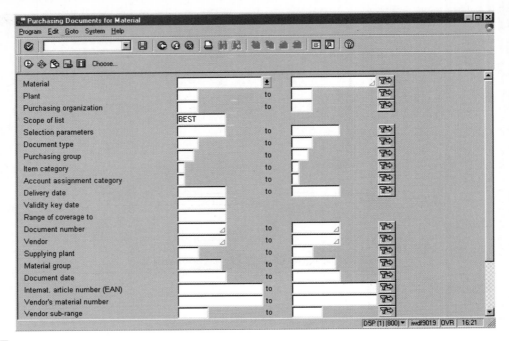

FIGURE 11.9 Specify your selection criteria here

The displayed window, MULTIPLE SELECTION FOR MATERIAL (see Figure 11.10) is similar in layout to the windows you know from the previous section. Maybe you already noticed the MULTIPLE SELECTION button in the earlier examples. We can make good use of this button now, to accept nearly two hundred materials into the selection at a stroke.

4 Click on MULTIPLE SELECTION.

The window shown in Figure 11.11 is displayed, and you specify the material type 'Finished products' in it.

TIP | THE MATERIAL TYPE FIELD ISN'T THERE?

In this case you first have to choose the material type as search help. Click on the symbol ▣ (CHOOSE SEARCH HELP). Then in the displayed window choose the search help 'Material type', and press (Return).

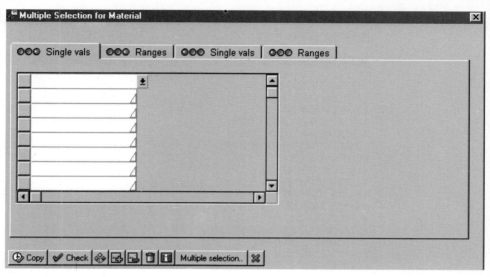

FIGURE 11.10 Starting in multiple selection for materials

5 In the 'Material type' field, enter the abbreviation 'FIN', which stands for the material type 'Finished products'. Then press (Return).

The displayed hit list contains all finished products present in your system (see Figure 11.12). You can already tell by the slider box that it is a pretty long list.

6 Click on 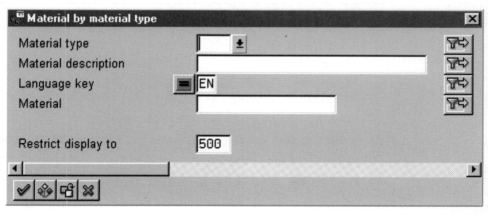 (SELECT ALL), to choose all the entries in the list, and then on ✔.

FIGURE 11.11 Search for materials using the material type

		Language	Material
Material type	FERT		
Material description			
☐ <TEST> IDESNORM 100-200		EN	ZJP-100
☐ 50 FLEX WIRE & CABLE		EN	S01
☐ 50 FLEX WIRE&CABLE		EN	FLEX WIRE CABLE
☐ A&D AIRCRAFT PROTOTYPE		EN	A-0001
☐ A&D AIRCRAFT PROTOTYPE		EN	IAD-1000
☐ ADMINISTRAÇÃO DE SISTEMA		EN	FORUM-010
☐ AEROSTAR 1200		EN	AEROSTAR
☐ AIR CONDITIONING		EN	AZ2-600
☐ ALUMINIUM WHEEL 7,5 * 17 "		EN	AS-101
☐ AS-100 T-SHIRT		EN	88
☐ AS-100 T-SHIRT		EN	89
☐ AUTO BLUE COLOR		EN	CO-01VI
☐ AUTO BOD STYLE MODEL 100		EN	BW-01VI
☐ AUTO CRUISE CONTROL		EN	CR-01VI
☐ AUTO ENGINE 1.8 LITER		EN	EN-02VI
☐ AUTO ENGINE 200 PS		EN	EN-01VI
☐ AUTO EXHAUST		EN	EX-01VI
☐ AUTO GEARBOX FOUR-SPEED DRIVE		EN	GB-01VI
☐ AUTO GOLF CL		EN	I4711
☐ AUTO HEADLIGHT STANDARD		EN	HL-01VI
☐ AUTO SHIPMENT PART		EN	SHIP
☐ AUTO SHOCK ABSORBER		EN	SA-01VI
☐ AUTO WHEEL		EN	WH-01VI
☐ AVUI PLOU		EN	548
☐ BAKERY PRODUCT; CONFIGURED TO ORDER		EN	JOSHPPPI1
☐ BASIC MOTOR 90KW		EN	T12345
☐ BILHETE 1ª PLATEIA		EN	CHAILLY-001
☐ BILHETE 2ª PLATEIA		EN	CHAILLY-002
☐ BILHETE BALCÃO CENTRAL		EN	CHAILLY-003

FIGURE 11.12 It's quite simple to choose all these entries at once

You return to the window MULTIPLE SELECTION FOR MATERIAL. The numbers of all finished products are now entered in the SINGLE VALUES tab page. SAP R/3 also shows you the number of entries, 393 in our example (Figure 11.13)!

7 Click on COPY to return to the selection window.

8 In the selection window, click as usual on ⊕ to generate the report.

Figure 11.14 shows the result.

9 Click on ⇐ until you see the SAP R/3 start window again.

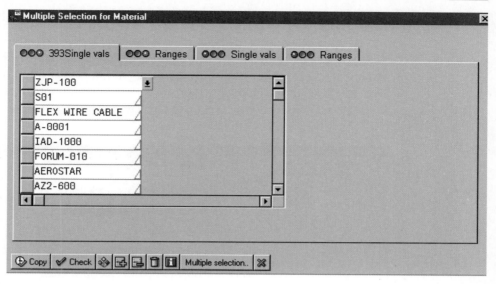

FIGURE 11.13   Nearly four hundred values entered at once!

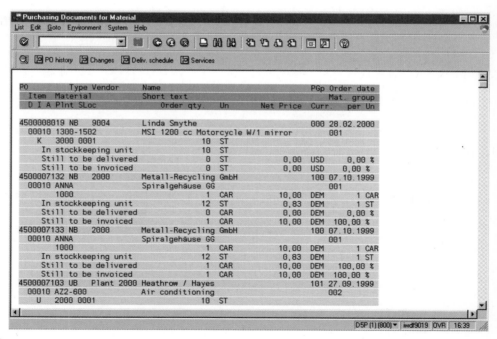

FIGURE 11.14   These are the purchasing documents for the finished products

THE INFORMATION SYSTEM – ALL REPORTS AT A GLANCE

Have you already noticed the INFORMATION SYSTEMS menu in the SAP R/3 start window (Figure 11.15)? You can call all the reports that SAP R/3 has to offer from here. You have all the reports in view, and can get on with report generation as soon as you start SAP R/3, without having to navigate to an application area first.

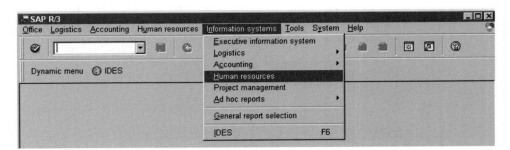

FIGURE 11.15 Entry into the information system

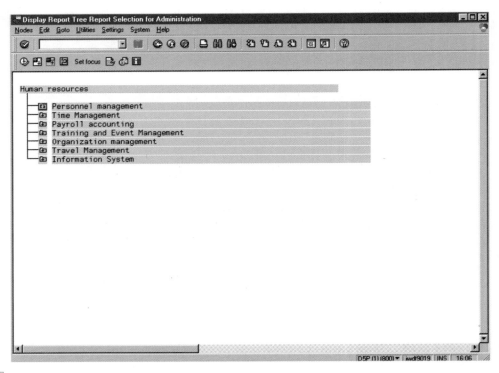

FIGURE 11.16 Reports in a tree structure

How to generate a report from the information system

1 Begin in the SAP R/3 start window. Choose INFORMATION SYSTEMS | HUMAN RESOURCES, and click in the displayed window on ⊞ (REPORT TREE).

You will see the window shown in Figure 11.16.

The reports in the *HR* area are arranged in a tree structure, just like the files and folders in the Windows Explorer. A click on ⊞ will display the next level in each case.

2 Open up the report tree under PERSONNEL MANAGEMENT | RECRUITMENT | APPLICANTS | TRAINING (see Figure 11.17).

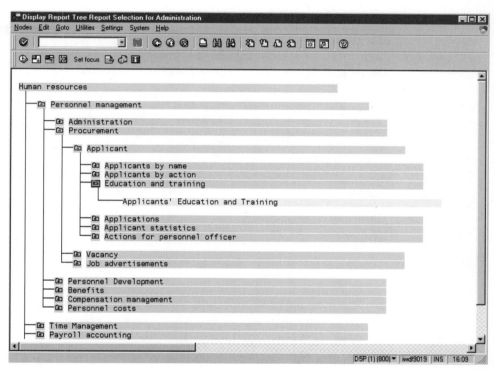

FIGURE 11.17 Reports on applicants in the information system

3   Double-click the report 'Applicants' Education and training'.

The subsequent selection window, APPLICANTS' EDUCATION AND TRAINING, looks much like the selection window VARIABLE APPLICANT LIST, which you know from the previous sections.

4   Drag down the slider box on the right margin until you see the lower part of the window. Do you see how this differs from the selection window in the previous sections? This selection window also contains fields with which you can choose applicants according to their training (see Figure 11.18).

However, in this example we are choosing the applicants only according to the receipt of their job application.

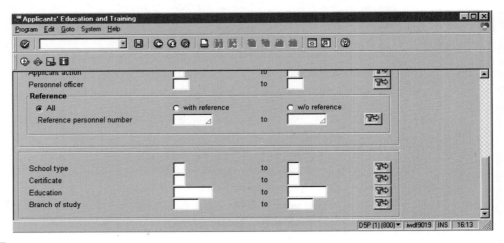

FIGURE 11.18   Selection of applicants according to their training

5   Show the upper window area again. In the fields 'Receipt of application' and 'To', enter the period for which you want to display the incoming job applications, e.g. from 01/01/1984 to 01/25/1999.

6   Click on 🕹 to generate the report.

We did it, and the received job applications are displayed! As you can see in Figure 11.19, this report supplies all the stored information on the applicants' training.

In this chapter you learned about various ways of using reports to obtain relevant information. In the next chapter you will find out how you can save selection criteria as *Variants*, and thereby make report generation even simpler.

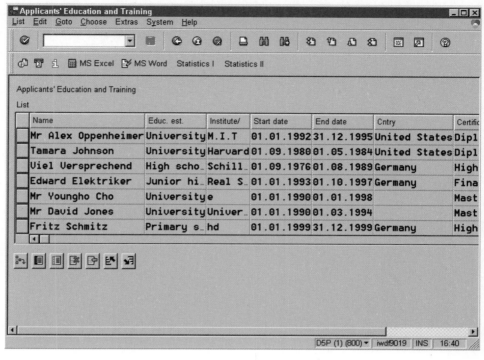

FIGURE 11.19   Information on the applicants' training

Always start report with the same selection criteria: Variants make this possible

In the last chapter you learned how to use reports to keep track of your data. You used selection criteria to specify the scope of a report, i.e. the quantity and nature of the data.

Reports should be as short as possible, in order to minimize the load on the SAP R/3 system from report generating, and to provide you with an easily comprehensible listing of your data. By specifying appropriate selection criteria you can set very precise limits on the data to be displayed. Such a list of selection criteria can also become pretty long and complex. In this case, it pays to save the selection criteria as a variant.

Variant

A variant is a group of saved selection criteria. A variant is created once and can subsequently be used repeatedly in report generation. You can save a lot of time with variants, since you do not have to compile your selection criteria from scratch for each report. Your variants are also available to other users, so your colleagues will benefit as well.

12.1 CREATING VARIANTS

Let's take a simple example. You work in the HR department and, from time to time, you would like to obtain an overview of the applicants for whom you are responsible. The first and last names, applicant number and date of application are all you need. You can save these selection criteria as a variant.

How to create a variant

1   Start SAP R/3, and log on to the training client.

2   Choose HUMAN RESOURCES | PERSONNEL MANAGEMENT | RECRUITMENT, to display the RECRUITMENT window.

3   In the RECRUITMENT window choose EVALUATIONS | VAR. APPLICANT LIST.

You will see the VARIABLE APPLICANT LIST selection window that you already know from the previous chapter (Figure 12.1).

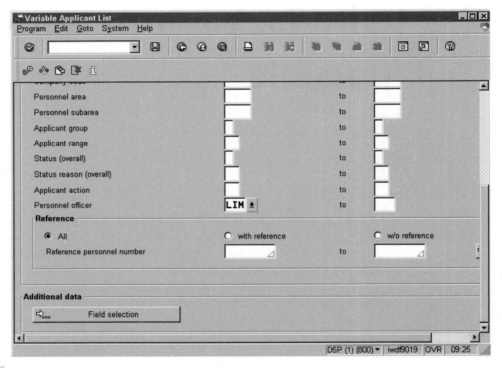

| **FIGURE 12.1** | Starting in the selection window |

4   In the 'Personnel officer' field, enter the abbreviation for an administrator. We use the abbreviation 'LIM' in the example. Use the value help to choose an abbreviation that you can use.

5   Click on FIELD SELECTION to display the HR FIELD SELECTION window. Choose the fields 'Applicant number' 'Last name', 'First name' and 'Application date' for the display. Do you remember how that's done? In the list of fields you can select, click on the button left of the field, and then on ▶.

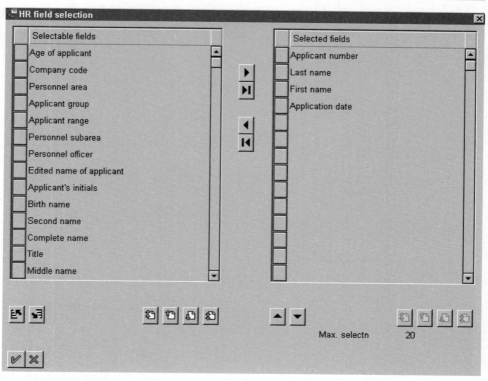

FIGURE 12.2   Selected fields

Compare the HR FIELD SELECTION window once more with Figure 12.2.

6   Press (Return) to return to the selection window. This should look something like Figure 12.3.

7   Click on [SAVE icon] (SAVE) to store the selection criteria as a variant.

The window ABAP: SAVE AS VARIANT appears.

8   Enter a name for the variant in the field 'Variant name'. The name can consist of any characters except the percentage sign % and dollar sign $. Enter a description of the variant in the field 'Description'. Just use the data from Figure 12.4.

9   Click on [save icon]. SAP R/3 informs you that the variant was saved (see Figure 12.5).

10   If information messages are shown in a separate dialog box for you, confirm the message with OK.

11   Click on [back arrow] to return to the previous window.

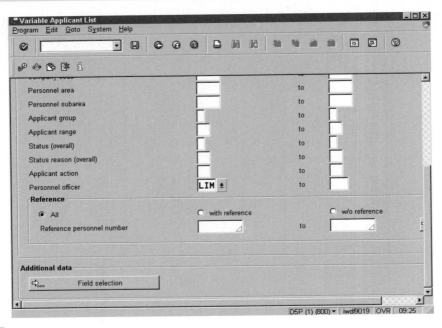

FIGURE 12.3 Selection criteria for the variant

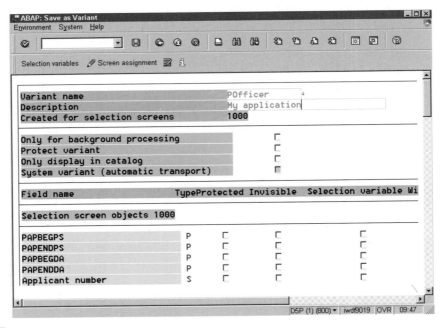

FIGURE 12.4 Give name and description for a variant

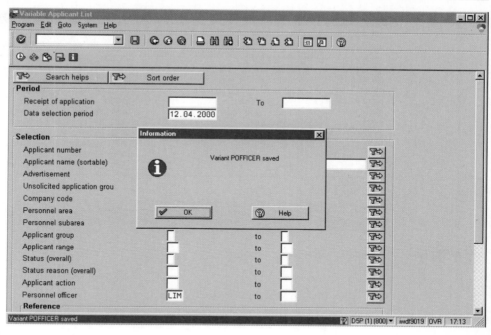

FIGURE 12.5   Success: the variant is saved

12.2   **USING VARIANTS**

Now that you have stored the variant, you can use it right away for report generation.

How to use a variant

1   The starting point is the RECRUITMENT window. You can get to this from the SAP R/3 start window via HUMAN RESOURCES | PERSONNEL MANAGEMENT | RECRUITMENT.

2   In the RECRUITMENT window choose EVALUATIONS | VAR. APPLICANT LIST.

3   Click on 🔲 (GET VARIANT).

You will see a list of all variants that you can use for your report. The list includes the variant you have just stored, and may also contain other variants (Figure 12.6).

4   Double-click on your variant.

You will return to the selection window. The selection criteria that are stored in the variant are now entered in the selection window.

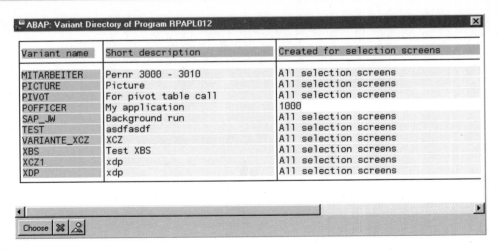

FIGURE 12.6
Available variants for a report

5 Click on to generate the report.

Figure 12.7 shows the report that was generated with the criteria used in our example.

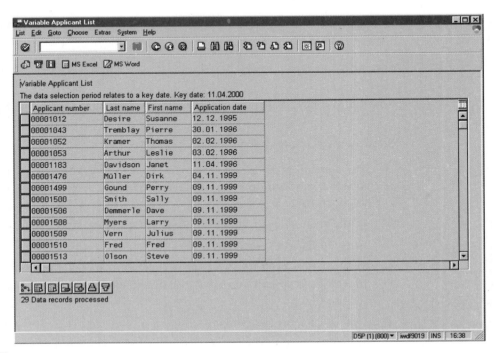

FIGURE 12.7
The generated report

You learned in this chapter how to simplify report generation with variants. In the next chapter you will learn how to postpone the generation of extensive reports to a later time, by creating an order. To do this you need the variant created in this chapter.

CHAPTER 13

Your order is being carried out: Background processing

So far, you have generated all reports interactively; in other words, you started report generation, and the SAP R/3 system found the data you requested and displayed it on your screen.

Background processing

Very extensive reports should be generated in background processing rather than interactively. In background processing, SAP R/3 starts report generation automatically, relieving you of the task. You only have to create an order, and tell SAP R/3 the date and time when the report should be generated. In addition, you specify print options for the report. Orders are often also called *Jobs*.

Your advantage: If you have the report generated in the background, you can continue working at once. The session with which you are currently working is not blocked by report generation. You can also selectively postpone report generation to times when the SAP R/3 system is less busy. Have a nice weekend and leave the work to the SAP R/3 system!

Do you have to generate regular reports, such as the open unpaid invoices at the end of the month? No problem: with background processing you can create orders that are started regularly.

Reports that take a long time to generate can be handled much faster in background processing. Some reports are therefore automatically forwarded to background processing with no need for you to create an order. Your system administration has already relieved you of work here. If you want to know when your job will be done, you have only to display the job status.

13.1 CREATING AN ORDER

Let's take the example of the report from Chapter 12, for which you created a variant. We will now apply this variant. When you create an order for a report, thereby making use of background processing, you have to specify a variant. This lets SAP R/3 know which selection criteria apply for the report generation.

When creating the order you also have to specify which ABAP program should be executed. So first you are going to learn the easy way to find out the name of the correct ABAP program.

TIP | **REMEMBER?**

A report is actually an ABAP program that fetches the necessary data from a database.

How to create an order

1 Start SAP R/3, and log on to the training client.

2 Choose HUMAN RESOURCES | PERSONNEL MANAGEMENT | RECRUITMENT, to call the RECRUITMENT window.

3 In the RECRUITMENT window choose EVALUATIONS | VAR. APPLICANT LIST.

You already know the VARIABLE APPLICANT LIST selection window from the previous chapters.

4 To create an order for the report, you first need the name of the ABAP program. Simply click on the name of the SAP R/3 system in the status bar. You can see the name of the ABAP program in the displayed menu (see Figure 13.1). Make a note of the program name.

5 Click on a free space in the selection window, to close the menu.

6 Now for the creation of your first order. Choose SYSTEM | SERVICES | JOBS | DEFINITION.

The DEFINE BACKGROUND JOB window is displayed.

7 Give a name for your job, and set 'C' as the job class.

TIP | **WHAT IS THE JOB CLASS?**

The job class decides the priority for job execution. You normally enter job class C (normal priority). System administration can also assign job classes A and B. Class B jobs take precedence over those of class C. Class A jobs take precedence over all other jobs.

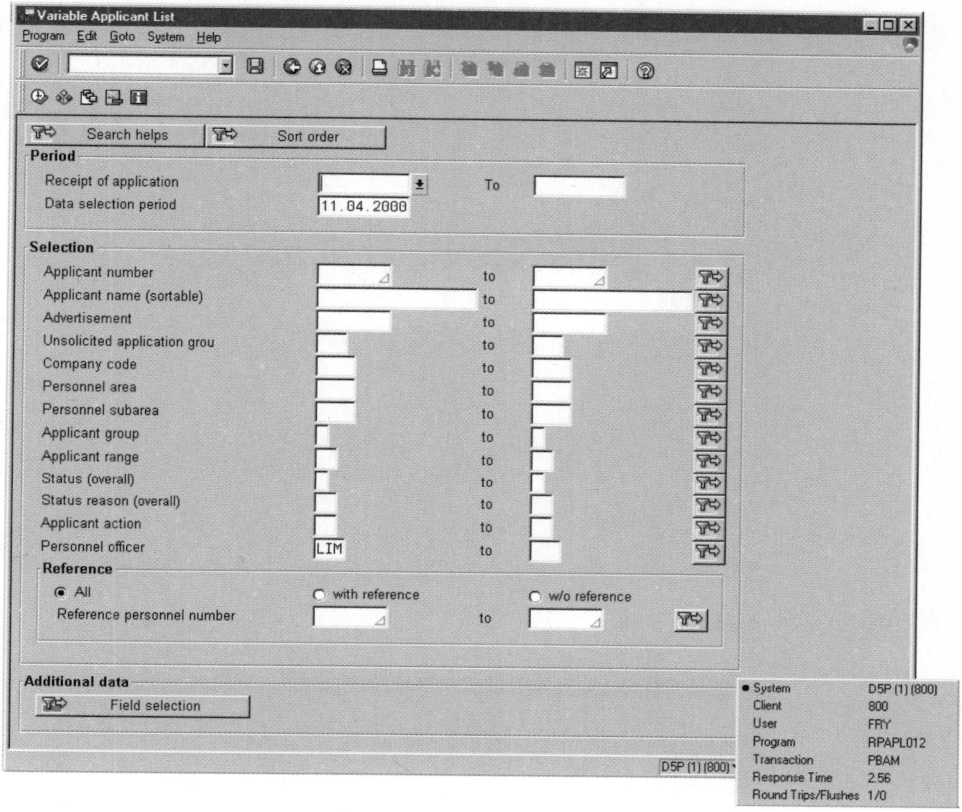

FIGURE 13.1   How to find out the name of an ABAP program

The window should look like Figure 13.2.

8 Next, you tell SAP R/3 which report the job is being created for. Click on STEPS for this.

The window CREATE STEP 1 is displayed (see Figure 13.3).

9 Click on ABAP PROGRAM.

10 Enter the ABAP program name that you noted earlier.

11 In the 'Variant' field, enter 'Officer'. This is the name of the variant you created in the previous chapter.

You no longer know the name of the variant? Just click on VARIANT LIST and choose the correct variant from the displayed list.

Then check whether the window looks like the one in Figure 13.3.

12 Save your inputs with 🖫.

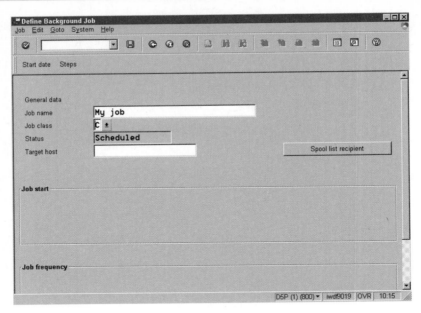

FIGURE 13.2 Creating a job

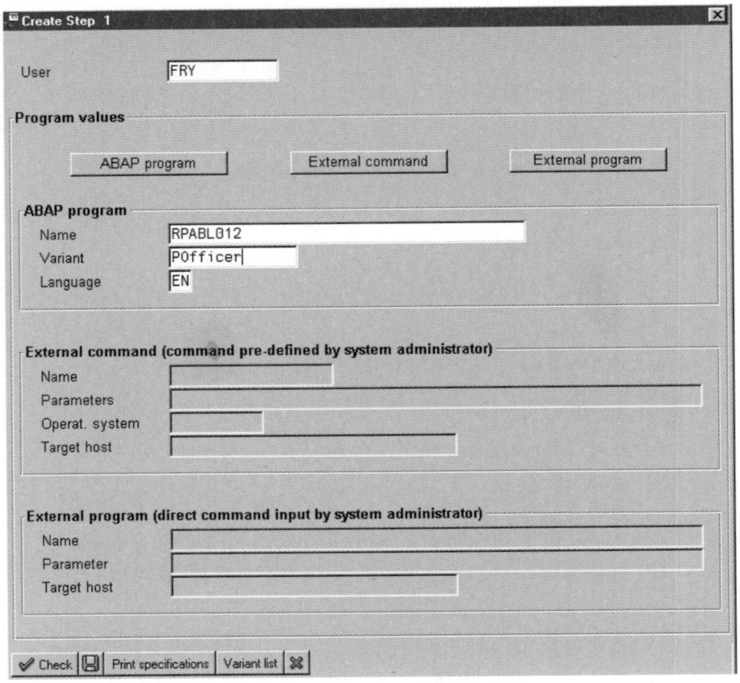

FIGURE 13.3 Specify ABAP program and variant

The window EDIT A STEP LIST is displayed; you can simply exit it with 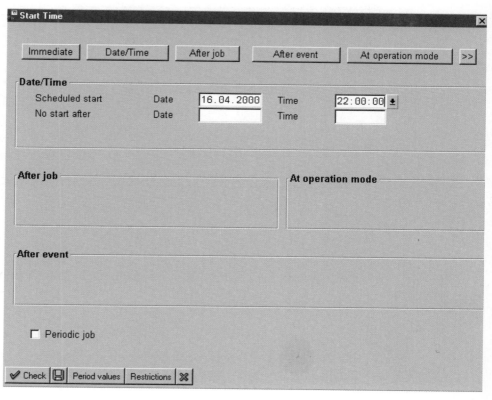. You will see the DEFINE BACKGROUND JOB window again.

13 Now click on START to specify when the job should be started.

The START TIME window is displayed.

14 Click on DATE/TIME. Specify, for example, that your job should be started on the following Sunday at 22:00. Figure 13.4 shows the window with the values for this example.

FIGURE 13.4 Specify date and time

TIP **YOU WANT TO GENERATE A REPORT EVERY MONTH?**

Simply create a job that is run regularly once a month. Consult the Introduction to SAP R/3 about this, by choosing the function INTRODUCTION TO R/3 in the HELP menu. Scroll through the Table of Contents to Background processing, and click on 'Scheduling background jobs'.

15 Click on 🖫 to save the inputs. You will see the DEFINE BACKGROUND JOB window again (Figure 13.5). You can check the date and time once more under START DATE.

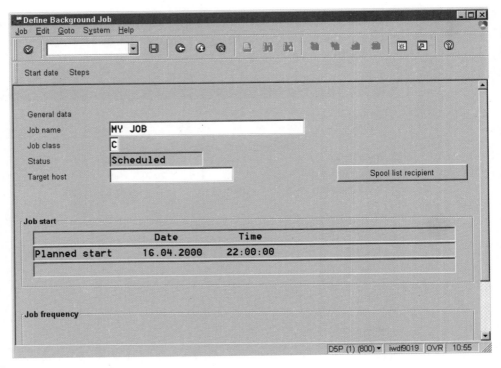

FIGURE 13.5   Check job definition one more time

16 Click on 🖫. SAP R/3 tells you that your job was saved.

17 Exit the window by clicking on ⬅ or 🔼.

13.2   IS THE JOB BEING PROCESSED?

An order (job) is not executed until it has been released. If you have the corresponding rights, your order is automatically released. Otherwise you have to consult your system administrator about release.

Now that you have created an order, it's best to check its status at once. Then you can see immediately whether your job has been released.

How to check the job status

1 You can start in any SAP R/3 window. Choose SYSTEM | OWN JOBS.

You will get a summary of the status of your jobs (orders). You can see in Figure 13.6 that one released job is present. That is the job we have just defined.

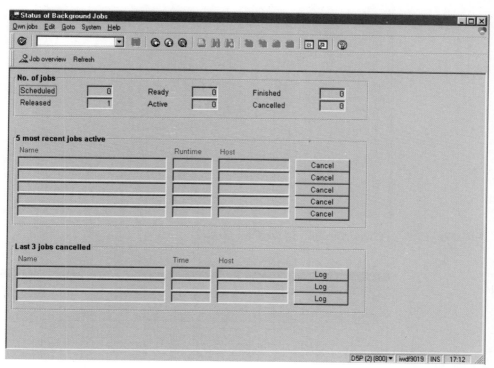

FIGURE 13.6   This window shows the status of your orders (jobs)

2 Would you like to see the data for your job again? Then click on 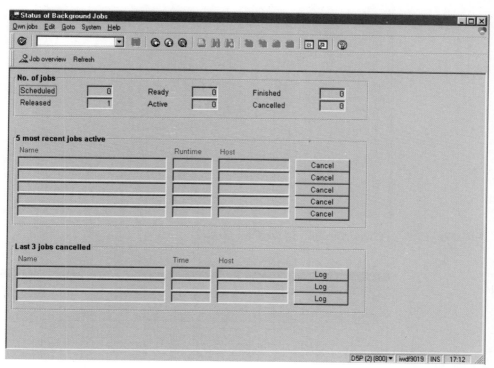 JOB SUMMARY.

You will get a selection window, in which you specify selection criteria for your jobs (see Figure 13.7).

3 Enter under 'Start date' the period in which the jobs are being started. For example, the window in Figure 13.7 shows date and time entries that are suitable for the job created in the previous section.

4 Press (Return).

You will see the list of your jobs that meet the selection criteria. Figure 13.8 shows an example. To look at details of one job, click on the order and then on &.

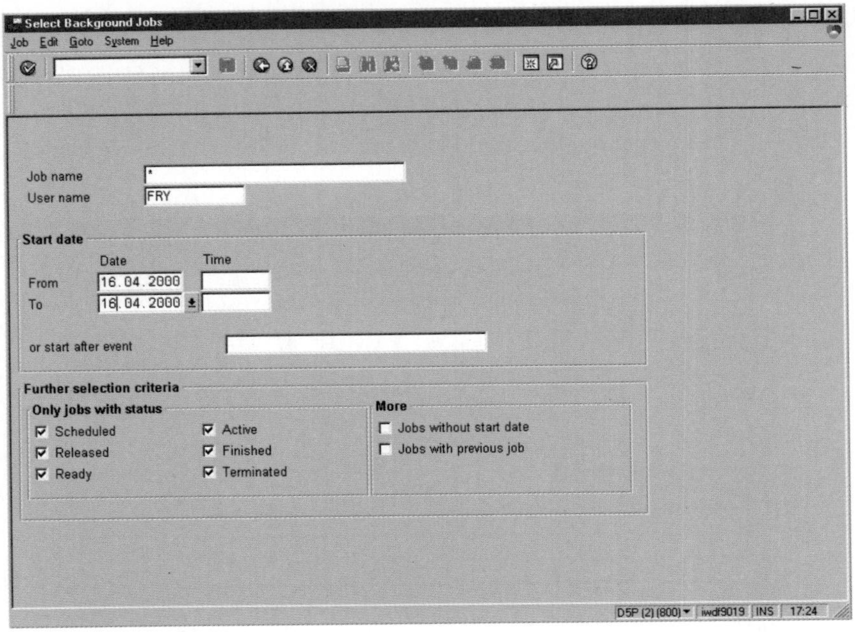

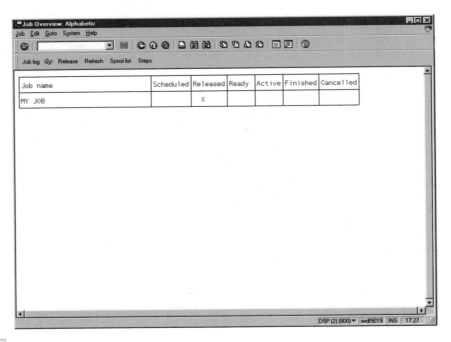

FIGURE 13.7   Which jobs do you want to display?

FIGURE 13.8   List of your jobs

TIP   **JOB CREATED IN ERROR?**

Don't worry, you can always delete an order created in error, as long as the job is not started. To do so you must display the window shown in Figure 13.8, JOB OVERVIEW: ALPHABETIC. Click on the job, and then choose JOB | DELETE. SAP R/3 asks if you really want to delete the job. Confirm with YES.

But you can also cancel a job that is actually active, by going to the window shown in Figure 13.6, OWN JOBS. Click on the active job, and then choose CANCEL.

5   Click on 🔼 until you see the SAP R/3 start window again.

In this chapter you created an order (job) for background processing. You also learned how to check the status of your jobs, and how to delete or stop incorrectly created orders. In the next chapter you will find out how to print your reports.

CHAPTER 14

Getting it in black and white: Printing reports

You do not actually need to print any reports at all. The data is clearly presented on screen for you, and what is printed today can already be out of date tomorrow. On screen you can always see the latest data. However, if you still want to have your reports in black and white occasionally, you will find out how in this chapter.

TIP   HOW CAN I PRINT THE CURRENT WINDOW?

Suppose you are busy entering an applicant's data, and would like to print out the current window with the data. No problem. If you have a computer with Windows 95, Windows 98 or Windows NT, simply choose ⬛ | PRINT SCREEN.

14.1   PRINT REPORT IMMEDIATELY

Once you have created a report, you can print it out immediately afterwards.

How to print a report immediately

1 Start SAP R/3, and log on to the training client.

2 Proceed as described in Section 11.1, 'Your first report', to generate a report. Figure 14.1 shows approximately how your report might look.

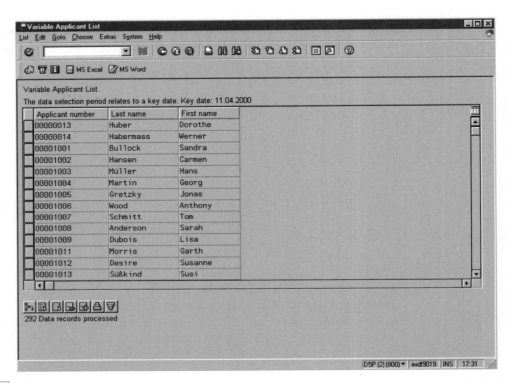

| **FIGURE 14.1** | First generate a report |

3 Click in the standard toolbar on 🖨.

The PRINT PARAMETERS window is displayed (see Figure 14.2).

4 Enter the name of your printer in the 'Output device' field. If you do not know the name by heart, you can find it with value help.

5 Mark 'Print immed.' to have the report printed at once. If 'New spool request' is selected, disable the option. The fields under 'Spool control' should look like those in Figure 14.2. The system administration has already correctly adjusted the other settings, in particular for the cover sheets and the output format, so you don't need to change anything here.

Print Parameters				✕
Output device			±	
Number of copies	1			

Spool request

Name	RPAPL012_FRY
Title	
Authorization	

Spool control

☐ Print immed.
☐ Delete after print
☑ New spool request
Retention period   8 Day(s)
Archiving mode   Print ±

Cover sheets

D SAP cover sheet
☐ Selection cover sheet
Recipient   FRY
Department

Output format

Lines	65
Columns	69
Format	

Set default value

FIGURE 14.2   Specify print parameters

6   Click on 🖨.

14.2   LONG REPORTS, MULTIPLE PRINTING? A SPOOL REQUEST DOES IT

Suppose you have generated a very long report, and actually want to print the report. But you do not want to monopolize the department printer, since your colleague has very urgent outstanding invoices to print. The best thing is to send your report to the output controller in the meantime. You can print it out from there later, when the printer isn't so busy.

You do not yet know exactly how many printed copies of your report will be needed? No problem. As long as the report is in the output controller, you can also print more copies of the report later.

Spool request

If you do not print a report immediately, you begin by generating a spool request. The data to be printed is stored in the spool request along with the information needed by SAP R/3 for printing it out.

Output controller   The spool request is sent to the output controller and can be printed from there later. The output controller is a program that runs on a central computer and collects all spool requests.

How to generate a spool request

1   If you did the last exercise, the report shown in Figure 14.1 should still be visible on your screen. If not, generate the report as described in Section 11.1, 'Your first report'.

2   Choose LIST | PRINT | STANDARD LIST.

You get the PRINT PARAMETERS window again, which you already saw in the previous section.

3   Enter the name of your printer in the 'Output device' field, or choose it using value help.

TIP   **MUST I SPECIFY MY PRINTER EVERY TIME?**

In SAP R/3 you can store default parameters for your user ID, to spare yourself some typing. You will find out in the next section how it is done. If you specify your printer as default, for example, it is automatically entered in the PRINT PARAMETERS window. If you want to use a different printer you can simply change the suggested printer.

---

4   Enter a description of the spool request under 'Title'. Make the description as informative as possible to help you to find your spool request later in the output controller.

5   Mark 'New spool request'. If you choose 'Delete after print', the spool request is deleted from the output controller as soon as it has been printed. You won't be able to print any more copies in this case.

If you do not click on 'Delete after print', the spool request remains for a while in the output controller. You can specify, in the 'Retention period' field, how many days later the spool request should be deleted. As long as the spool request is still in the output controller, you can print further copies. Figure 14.3 shows an example of how the options for a spool request might look.

6   Click on 🖶.

A message informs you that your spool request has been passed to the output controller.

In order to print the report, you must now display the output controller.

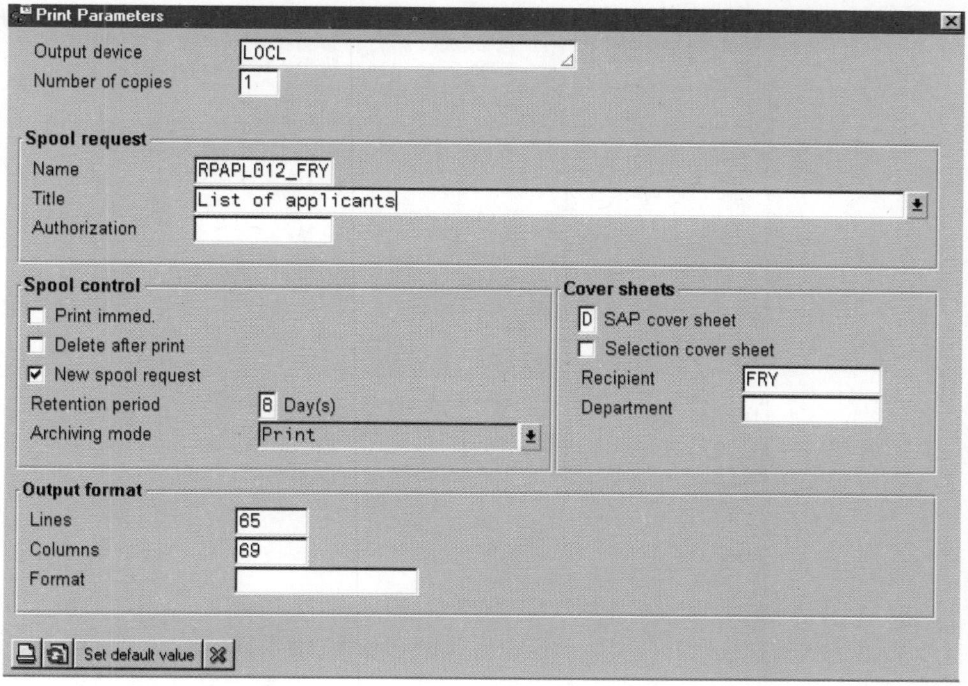

FIGURE 14.3 Print options for a spool request

14.3 SPOOL REQUESTS – A CASE FOR THE OUTPUT CONTROLLER

The output controller collects all the spool requests that are submitted to it. To print a spool request, you display the output controller and can then start the printing.

How to print from the output controller

1   You can call the output controller from any window. Choose SYSTEM | SERVICES | OUTPUT CONTROLLER.

The window SPOOL: REQUEST SCREEN is displayed. The fields in this window are selection criteria with which the spool requests to be displayed can be more precisely delimited. Figure 14.4 shows, for example, which selection criteria are entered when the window is called. For this example you do not need to enter any further selection criteria.

2   Click on [icon] to display the spool requests.

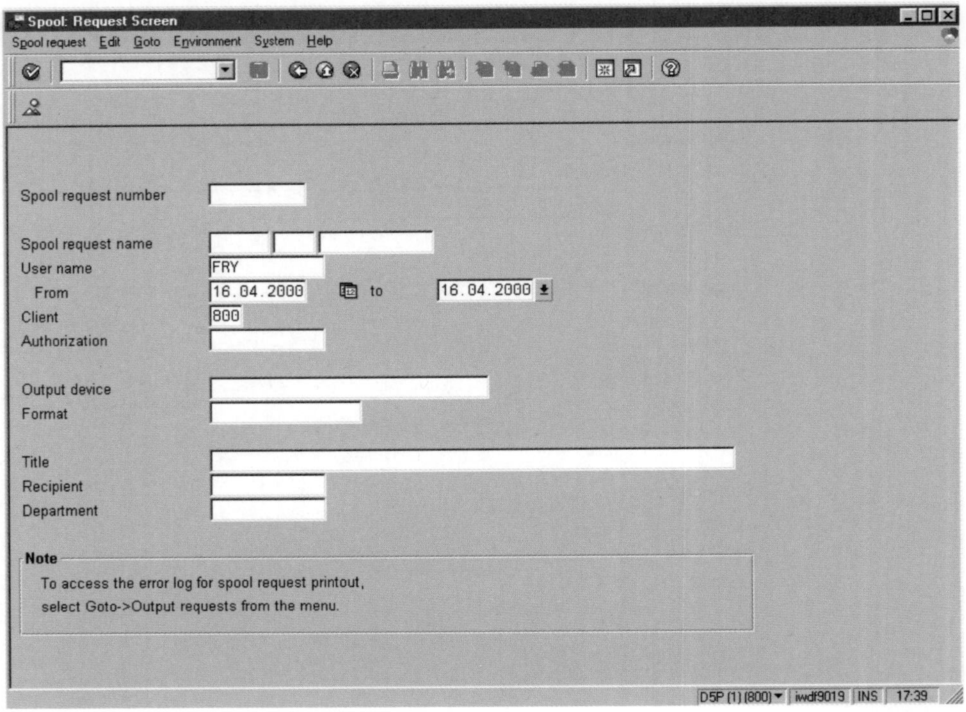

FIGURE 14.4   Which spool requests do you want to see?

A window appears with the list of your spool requests. In the window in Figure 14.5, the spool request generated in the previous example appears in the first line.

TIP   **IS THE LIST TOO LONG?**

Click on 🔍 to find the spool request. If you remember the title of the spool request, you can use part or all of it for the search.

---

3   To print the spool request, select it and click on 🖨.

The output controller has a lot more to offer. For instance, you can preview how your data will look on paper, and change the number of prints. You can delete spool requests from the output controller when you no longer need them. You will find more information on the output controller in the SAP R/3 Online Help.

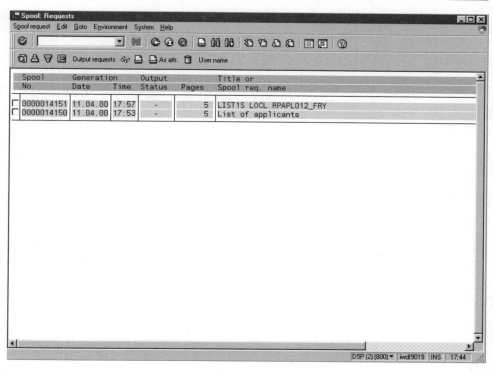

FIGURE 14.5 List of the spool requests

SPECIFYING PERSONAL PRINT SETTINGS

Do you generally print your data with the same printer? Then it is better to store the printer as a default parameter. These default parameters apply for you personally, i.e. for your user ID. Your colleagues can have different default parameters.

How to save default parameters for printing

1 You can start from any SAP R/3 window. Choose SYSTEM | USER PROFILE | OWN DATA.

2 Click in the displayed window on the tab page USER DEFAULTS (see Figure 14.6).

3 Enter the printer with which you usually print under 'Output device'. If you are not sure of the name, you can choose it from the value help.

4 If you usually want your data to be output immediately, mark 'Output immediately'. If your spool requests should normally be deleted after printing, click on 'Delete after output'.

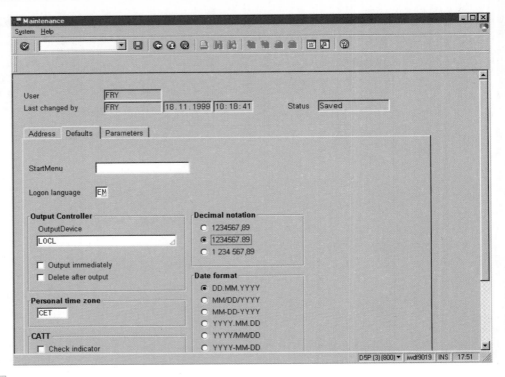

FIGURE 14.6   Default parameters for printing

5   Save your default parameters by clicking on 🖫.

The window MAINTENANCE of your own user profile is closed.

6   Why not try out your default parameters right away? Generate a report, and choose PRINT. Your default parameters are already entered in the displayed PRINT PARAMETERS window.

In this chapter you learned a few ways to print reports in SAP R/3. You also saw how to save time with default parameters when printing. In the next chapter you will find out how you can store default parameters for fields, and thereby cut down further on the typing.

CHAPTER 15

It's all in there: Default values for fields

You already know how to store default values for printing. It means you do not need to specify a printer for your print job, for instance. But SAP R/3 also offers you other options to save time.

Let's stay with the HR department example. Suppose you are dealing mainly with applicants who are interested in jobs with your firm in Berlin. You are primarily looking after those applying for executive employee positions. When entering the applicant data you can save yourself some typing work if you store default values for the relevant fields in SAP R/3.

User parameters

Default values for fields are called *User parameters* in SAP R/3. User parameters apply for you personally, i.e. for your user ID. Your colleagues may have saved other user parameters. Your user parameters will still be there next time you log on to SAP R/3. In other words, you do not have to specify them again each time you start SAP R/3.

15.1   WHICH FIELD?

Parameter ID

In SAP R/3 a field is usually assigned an identifier. This identifier enables SAP R/3 to distinguish the fields from one another. The identifier is known in SAP R/3 as a *Parameter ID*.

To save a default value for a field, you have to know the parameter ID for the field. For our example we will take the fields 'Applicant range' and 'Personnel area', which are filled in when applicant data is entered.

How to locate the parameter ID

1 Start SAP R/3, and log on to the training client.

2 In the start window choose HUMAN RESOURCES | PERSONNEL MANAGEMENT | RECRUITMENT once more. Click on INITIAL DATA ENTRY.

The INITIAL ENTRY OF BASIC DATA window is displayed (Figure 15.1).

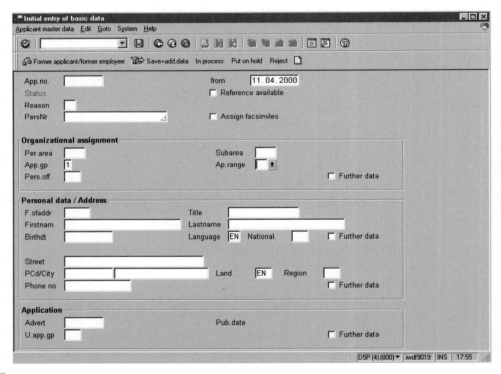

FIGURE 15.1 It starts here

3 Set the cursor in the field 'Per. area', and click on ![icon], or press (F1).

A help window with information on the field is displayed (see Figure 15.2).

4 Click on TECHNICAL INFO.

You will see the window shown in Figure 15.3. There you will find the parameter ID for the field.

```
Help - Initial entry of basic data                                          ☒

    Personnel area

        A personnel area is an organizational entity representing an area within
        an enterprise defined by specific aspects of personnel administration,
        time management and payroll.

        Personnel areas are subdivided into personnel subareas.




    ✔ 🔾 | Application help | Technical info | ✐ ☒
```

FIGURE 15.2   The help window takes you further

```
Technical Information                                                       ☒

┌─ Screen data ─────────────────────────────────────────────────┐
│   Program name      SAPMPAP4                                   │
│   Screen number     0100                                       │
└───────────────────────────────────────────────────────────────┘

┌─ GUI data ────────────────────────────────────────────────────┐
│   Program name      SAPMPAP4                                   │
│   Status            FAS1                                       │
└───────────────────────────────────────────────────────────────┘

┌─ Field data ──────────────────────────────────────────────────┐
│   Struct.           Q4000                                      │
│   Field name        WERKS                                      │
│   Data element      PERSA                                      │
│   DE supplement     0                                          │
│   Parameter ID      PBR                                        │
└───────────────────────────────────────────────────────────────┘

┌─ Field description for batch input ───────────────────────────┐
│   Scrn field        Q4000-WERKS                               │
└───────────────────────────────────────────────────────────────┘

✔ | Navigate | ☒
```

FIGURE 15.3   Find the parameter ID for a field

5 It is best to copy the parameter ID to the clipboard, so that you do not have to remember the identifier. Set the cursor in the field 'Parameter ID', and select the identifier, in this case 'PBR'. Press (Ctrl) + (C) to copy the identifier.

6 Close the TECHNICAL INFO by clicking on ✔. Close the help window in the same way.

7 To save a default value for the field 'Per. area' afterwards, you also need the value that you want to store as a default value. In this example we will take the value '1100', which stands for the personnel area Berlin.

8 Return with ⬅ to the SAP R/3 start window.

15.2 HOW YOU SPECIFY THE DEFAULT VALUES

You found the parameter ID, so the first step is done. Now it is a question of saving the default value.

How to save a default value for a field

1 You can start from any SAP R/3 window. Choose SYSTEM | USER PROFILE | OWN DATA.

2 Click in the displayed window on the tab page PARAMETERS.

You can enter your default values in the list you see there.

3 Set the cursor in the 'Parameters' field. If you copied the parameter ID to the clipboard, you can insert it right away. Press (Ctrl) + (V). The current contents of the clipboard are inserted. If you noted the parameter ID you can also type it in, of course.

4 Enter the default value in the 'Value' field. In this example we are taking the value '1100' for the personnel area Berlin. Compare your default values once more with Figure 15.4.

5 Save your inputs with 💾.

The window MAINTENANCE is closed. SAP R/3 informs you that your user ID was saved.

TIP CAN I DELETE A DEFAULT VALUE AGAIN?

If you no longer need a default value for a field, you can delete it again at any time.

Open the window MAINTENANCE. Click on the button to the left of the default value you want to delete. This action selects the entire line, and you can delete the line with 📝. Do not forget to save your changes with 💾.

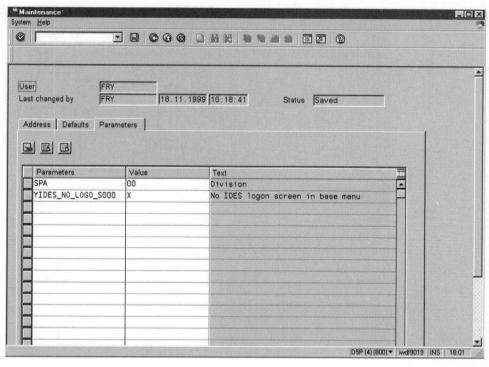

FIGURE 15.4 Your personal default values

6 Try it out now, to see whether the default value takes effect. Choose HUMAN RESOURCES | PERSONNEL MANAGEMENT | RECRUITMENT.

Can you see it? In the displayed INITIAL ENTRY OF BASIC DATA window, the personnel area is already present (see Figure 15.5).

7 Incidentally, you can store default values for as many fields as you wish. If you'd like to practise some more, you could save the entry 'Executive employee' as a default value for the 'Applicant range' field, for example. The process is exactly the same as with the default value for the personnel area.

8 When you've completed the exercise, click on ⬅ until you are back in the SAP R/3 start window.

In this chapter you learned how to save time with default values for fields. In the next chapter you will find out how to compile a Favourites list and choose your own start menu.

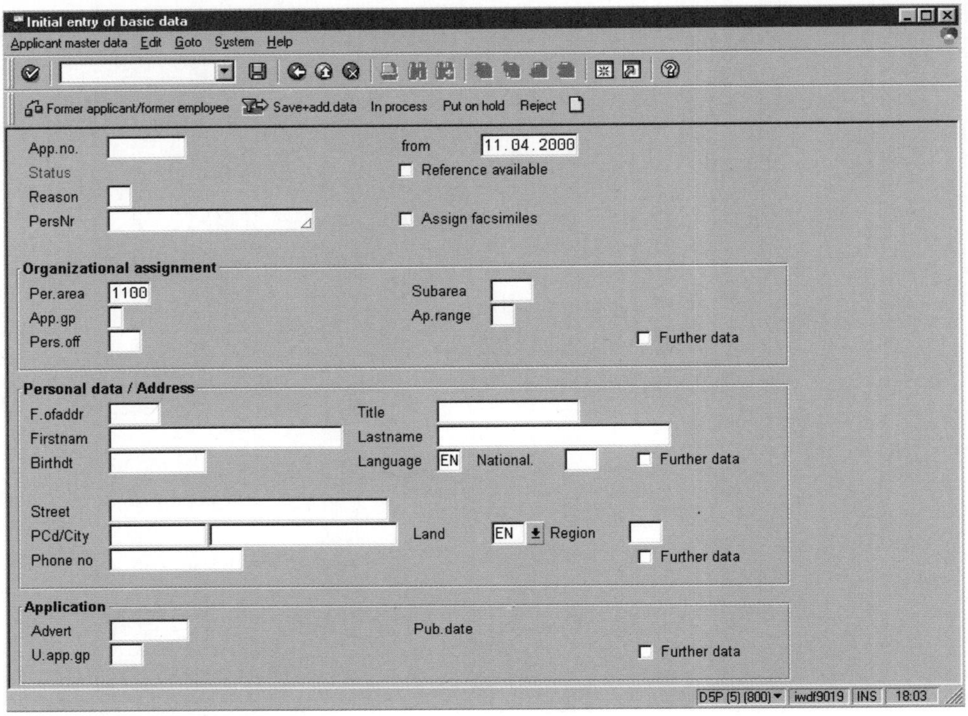

FIGURE 15.5 The personnel area is already there!

CHAPTER 16

Your personal settings: Favourites list and start menu

When you work with SAP R/3, you will call some applications quite frequently, and you will need others occasionally.

Wouldn't you like to have a list of the applications you use the most? With SAP R/3, you can easily compile just that.

16.1   THESE ARE YOUR FAVOURITES

You should include frequently used applications in your list of favourites. Your advantage: You do not need to remember the menus and submenus through which you get to these applications. Remember Chapter 9? You learned there how to use transaction codes to branch directly to an application. Transaction codes have one disadvantage, though: they are easily forgotten. You are on safer ground with your favourites list.

TIP   **YOU WORK WITH VERY FEW APPLICATIONS?**

Then your best plan is to create shortcuts on your Windows desktop. Look this up again in Chapter 9.

You can compile your favourites list entirely according to your wishes. Your favourites apply only to you personally. Other users can put together their own favourites.

How to compile your favourites

1 Start SAP R/3, and log on to the training client.

2 You can start in any window in SAP R/3. Choose SYSTEM | USER PROFILE | FAVOURITES MAINTENANCE.

The window shown in Figure 16.1 is displayed.

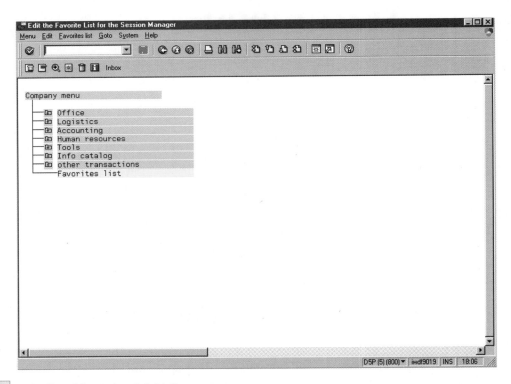

FIGURE 16.1 The list of favourites is initially empty

You are already familiar with the menu tree you see in the window. You will find the same menus and menu functions there as in the SAP R/3 start window – just presented differently. You can display the next level in each case by clicking on ⊞.

3 As an example we will add the initial entry of applicant data to the favourites list. Expand the menu tree successively under HUMAN RESOURCES until it looks like Figure 16.2.

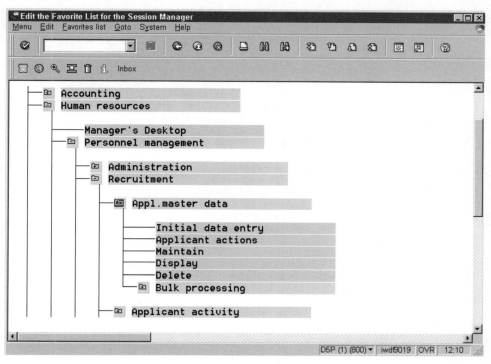

FIGURE 16.2   The expanded menu tree looks like this

4   In the expanded menu tree, click on 'Initial entry of basic data' and then on ![icon].

SAP R/3 informs you that an entry has been added to your favourites list.

5   Take a look at the result. Scroll down the window until you see the favourites list. The result should be as shown in Figure 16.3.

TIP   **DO YOU KNOW THE TRANSACTION CODES?**

If you know the transaction code for an application by heart, you can put together your favourites list even more quickly. Choose FAVORITES LIST | APPEND TRANSACTION in the menu bar. Enter the transaction code in the displayed window, and press (Return).

---

6   Extend your favourites list with further applications. When your list is complete, return to the SAP R/3 start window with ![icon].

7   Now your favourites are ready for action. When you see the SAP R/3 start window, click on DYNAMIC MENU.

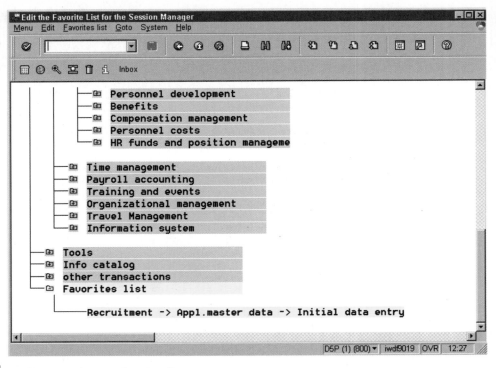

FIGURE 16.3   A first entry in your favorites list

You will see the window in Figure 16.4. The displayed menu tree contains your favourites list.

8   Double-click on the appropriate entry in the favourites list to start the application. You are immediately at your destination!

9   Return to the SAP R/3 start window with ⬅.

By the way, system administration can also compile a user menu for you. It can contain all the applications you work with, for example, or the applications you need the most.

How to display your user menu

1   Click in the SAP R/3 start window on DYNAMIC MENU.

2   Choose MENU | USER MENU.

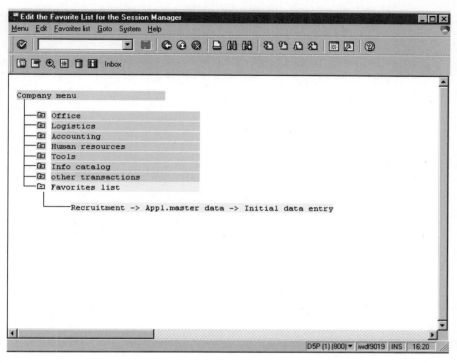

FIGURE 16.4   Your favorites are ready for action

WHICH MENU DO YOU START WITH?

If you work most of the time with the same menu, you can set this as the start menu. Then after you log on to the system, you are in the right place immediately.

Try the start menu using Recruitment as an example. First you have to find out what the required menu in SAP R/3 is called. Then you can set it as your start menu.

How to set your start menu

1   Start in the SAP R/3 start window. Choose HUMAN RESOURCES | PERSONNEL MANAGEMENT | RECRUITMENT.

   The RECRUITMENT window is displayed (Figure 16.5).

2   Choose SYSTEM | STATUS.

   You will see the window in Figure 16.6.

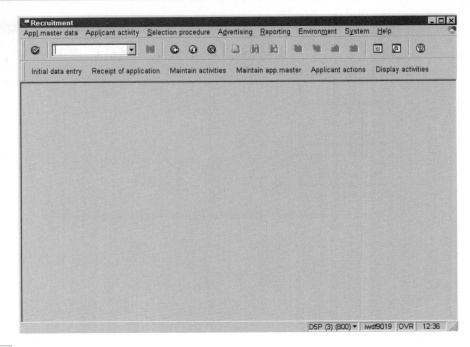

FIGURE 16.5 First display the right window...

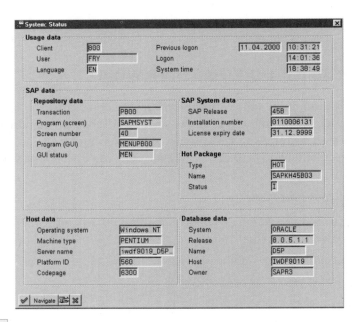

FIGURE 16.6 The menu name is shown here

The menu name is in the field 'Program(GUI)'. In this example, the menu name is 'MENUPB00'. Only 'PB00' is entered as the start menu, without the prefix 'MENU'.

3   It is best to copy 'PB00' to the clipboard so that you do not need to make a note of the name. Set the cursor in the field 'Program(GUI)' and select 'PB00'. Press (Ctrl) + (C) to copy the identifier.

4   Close the SYSTEM: STATUS window by clicking on ⬅.

5   You can set your start menu from any SAP R/3 window. Choose SYSTEM | USER PROFILE | OWN DATA.

6   Click in the displayed window on the tab page USER DEFAULTS.

7   Set the cursor in the 'Start menu' field. If you copied the name to the clipboard, press (Ctrl) + (V). The current contents of the clipboard are inserted. But you can also type the name directly into the field.

Figure 16.7 shows how your window should look.

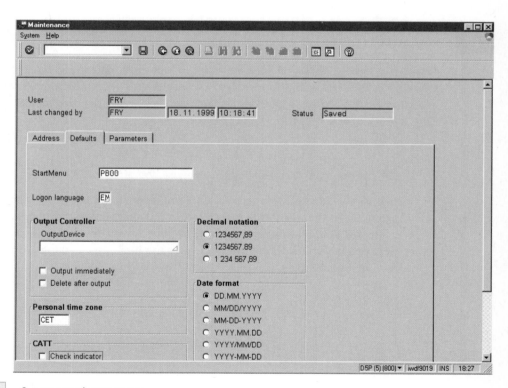

| FIGURE 16.7 | Set personal start menu |

TIP | **WHAT LANGUAGE SHOULD SAP R/3 START WITH?**

The SAP R/3 user interface is available in various languages. The system administration will usually have set the right language for you.

If not, you can easily do this yourself. Enter the abbreviation for the language you want in the field 'Logon language'. You can also use the value help if necessary, to find the right language code.

8 Save your inputs with ▐.

The window MAINTENANCE of your own user profile is closed. SAP R/3 informs you that your user ID was saved.

9 The start menu only becomes active with the next logon. Log off from SAP R/3, and then log on again.

After logon, SAP R/3 displays the RECRUITMENT window immediately.

TIP | **HOW DO I GET TO THE SAP R/3 START WINDOW?**

Have you tried to display the SAP R/3 start window with ⬅? If you have set a special start menu, this does not work. However, you can use the transaction code S000, which stands for the start window. Enter '/nS000' in the command field in the standard toolbar. You are back in the start window!

10 When you've completed the exercise, log off from SAP R/3.

It is always possible to specify a different start menu, or work without a start menu again. Open the window MAINTENANCE, and change the start menu as you wish.

In this chapter you learned how to store favourites and set a start menu. In the next chapter you will find out how you can tailor your working environment to your own requirements.

CHAPTER 17

As you like it: Configuring the working environment

SAP R/3 offers you all sorts of ways to set up your working environment exactly as you wish. You have already seen some of them:

- Personal print settings in Chapter 14
- Default parameters for fields in Chapter 15
- Start menu and logon language in Chapter 16

But these are by no means all the possibilities. In this chapter you will learn what other settings SAP R/3 has to offer. All the settings you will learn about in this chapter apply personally to you, i.e. to your user ID. Your settings do not affect other users. So you can feel free to try them out and see what suits you best.

17.1   DATE FORMAT AND DECIMAL NOTATION – SLASH, DOT OR COMMA?

In the examples so far we have given dates in the form MM/DD/YYYY, e.g. 01/01/1999. If you prefer a different date format, you can easily set this. Maybe you would rather have 1999/01/01. Similarly, you can specify a different decimal notation: decide whether you want to write a million in the form 1.000.000,00 or 1 000 000,00 or 1,000,000.00.

No matter what format you choose – in SAP R/3 you then have to enter all dates in the chosen format. And all numbers must be entered with the chosen decimal notation. However, it's no problem to change the date format and decimal sign at any time.

Your choices apply only to input and display in the user interface. SAP R/3 stores all dates and numbers internally in its own format.

How to choose date format and decimal notation

1 Start SAP R/3, and log on to the training client.

2 You can specify the settings from any SAP R/3 window. Choose SYSTEM | USER PROFILE | OWN DATA.

3 Click in the displayed window on the tab page USER DEFAULTS.

You will see the formats available for your choice in Figure 17.1.

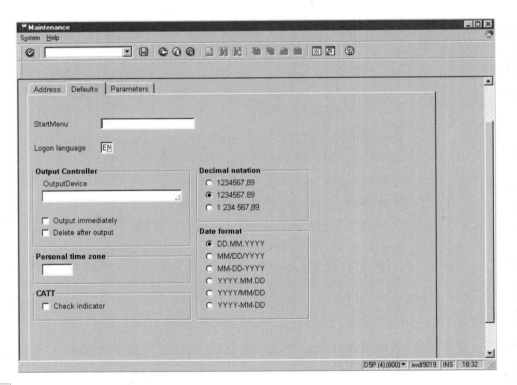

FIGURE 17.1   Date format and decimal notation

4 Choose what you want for the decimal notation and date format.

5 Save your inputs with 💾.

The window MAINTENANCE is closed. SAP R/3 informs you that your user ID was saved.

17.2 SAP R/3 WINDOW – WITH ALL THE TRIMMINGS

SAP R/3 offers you the chance to show or hide the standard toolbar, button bar and status bar. The best thing is to have all three bars showing.

How to show the standard toolbar, button bar and status bar

1   You can specify the settings from any SAP R/3 window. Click on 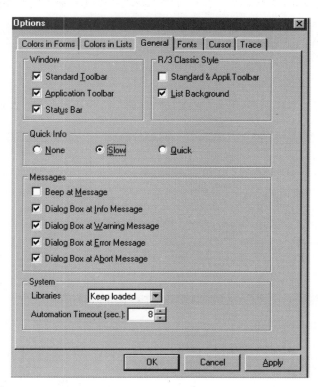 and then on OPTIONS.

2   Click in the displayed dialog box on the GENERAL tab page.

3   Under 'Window' you can choose to show the standard toolbar, button bar and status bar. The button bar is also referred to as the application toolbar in SAP R/3. The dialog box should look like that shown in Figure 17.2.

FIGURE 17.2 SAP R/3 offers numerous settings

4 Click on OK to save the changes.

The dialog box remains open and you can specify further settings.

TIP CLASSIC OR NOT?

With SAP R/3 you can even choose how the standard toolbar and the button bar should look. Figure 17.3 shows the difference between classic and non-classic style. It is classic if you enable the option 'Standard and Application Toolbar' under 'R/3 Classic Style'.

You also have a choice of background for lists. In classic style, lists are on a grey background. Otherwise the background is white. Give it a try, and see which you prefer.

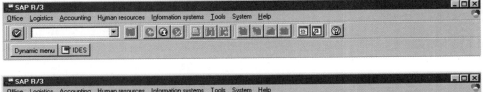

FIGURE 17.3 Classic or not classic – take your pick

17.3 MESSAGES – A SEPARATE WINDOW

You can choose how SAP R/3 brings messages to your attention. Messages can be displayed either only in the status bar or additionally in a separate message window. You can also have an alert tone sounded for error messages.

Messages in the status bar are easily overlooked. In comparison, if messages are displayed in a separate window, they are more conspicuous. In Figures 17.4 and 17.5 you can see both options once more. Choose the display that seems most useful to you.

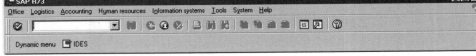

FIGURE 17.4 Message in the status bar...

How to display messages in a separate window

1 If the OPTIONS dialog box is not open, open it with 🔘 | OPTIONS.

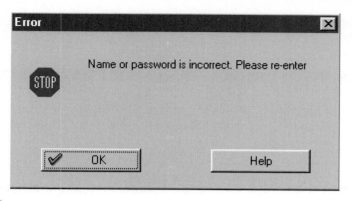

FIGURE 17.5 ...and in a separate window

2 Click on the GENERAL tab page.

3 Specify under 'Messages' which messages are to be displayed in a separate window (Figure 17.6). If you want to be alerted to messages by a warning tone, click on 'Beep at Message'.

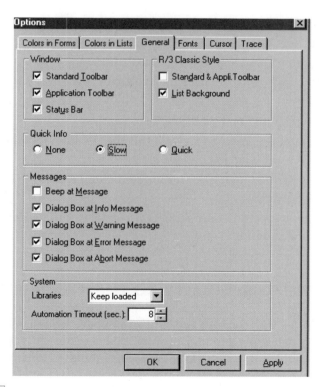

FIGURE 17.6 There are numerous settings for the SAP R/3 user interface

4 Click on OK to save the changes.

17.4 QUICK INFO – THE EXPLANATION FOR THE SYMBOL

Do you still remember Chapter 3? You learned there how to display a brief explanation (the so-called 'quick info') for a symbol. Figure 17.7 shows the example from Chapter 3 once more.

FIGURE 17.7 Quick info in the logon window

How to switch on quick info

1 If the OPTIONS dialog box is not open, open it with  | OPTIONS.

2 Click on the GENERAL tab page.

Specify under 'Quick info' that you want to see explanations for the symbols. You can choose whether to have the explanations displayed after a short delay, or immediately.

3 Try the setting 'slow', and click on OK.

4 Move the mouse pointer to a symbol in the standard toolbar, to try out the option.

5 Open the OPTIONS dialog box again, and change the Quick info setting to 'quick'. Click on OK.

6 Move the mouse pointer once more to a symbol in the standard toolbar, to try out the changed setting.

17.5 CURSOR – AUTOMATICALLY TO THE NEXT FIELD

Do you work mainly with the keyboard, and do you have to input a lot of data? Then you can speed up data entry enormously with optimal cursor settings.

Especially useful: You can specify that the cursor jumps automatically to the next input field as soon as the end of the current field is reached. Then there is no need to press the tab key after data input in a field.

Making the cursor jump automatically to the next field

1 You can make these settings from any SAP R/3 window. Click at the far right of the menu bar on 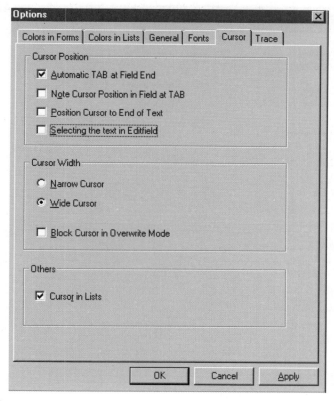 and then on OPTIONS.

2 Click in the displayed dialog box on the CURSOR tab page.

3 Click on 'Automatic TAB at Field End' (see Figure 17.8).

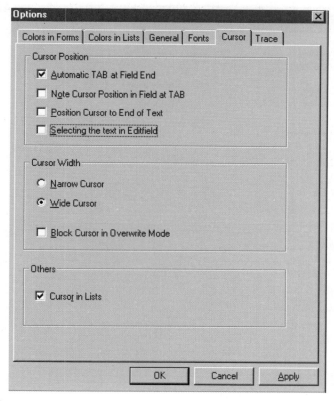

FIGURE 17.8 Optimal cursor setting

4 Click on OK to save the changes.

17.6 CURSOR – WHAT ELSE YOU CAN SET

You no doubt noticed that lots of other settings are possible in the CURSOR tab. In the next exercises you can try out the effects of the various settings.

SAP R/3 notes the cursor position

1 Display the window for entering applicant data: In the SAP R/3 start window choose HUMAN RESOURCES | PERSONNEL MANAGEMENT | RECRUITMENT. Then click on INITIAL ENTRY OF BASIC DATA.

2 In the fields 'Form of address' and 'Title', enter the data that you see in Figure 17.9.

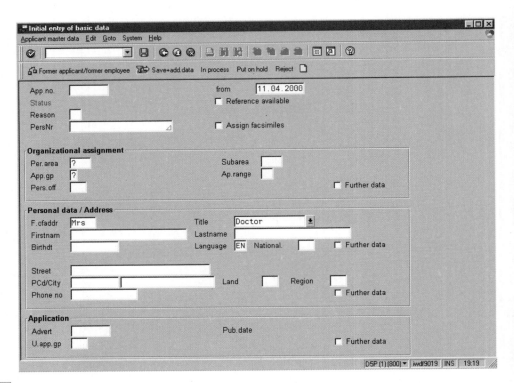

| **FIGURE 17.9** | Test settings for the cursor |

3 Now click on  and then on OPTIONS. In the displayed dialog box, click again on the CURSOR tab page.

4 Switch on the option 'Note Cursor Position in Field at TAB'. Click on OK.

5 In the 'Form of address' (F. ofaddr) field, set the cursor between r and s (as in Figure 17.10).

| **FIGURE 17.10** | Set the cursor in the middle of a field |

6   Press (Tab) to jump to the next field, and then (Shift) + (Tab), to jump back to the 'Form of address' field.

Have you noticed? The cursor is once more between the letters r and s. That is, SAP R/3 has noted the cursor position in the 'Form of address' field.

7   Now open the OPTIONS dialog box, and switch off the option 'Note cursor position in field at TAB'. Then click on OK. Repeat steps 5 and 6. This time the cursor jumps to the start of the field, i.e. SAP R/3 hasn't noted the position.

The cursor jumps automatically to end of text

1   We will stay with applicant data entry. Open the OPTIONS dialog box, and go to the CURSOR tab again.

2   Switch on the option 'Position Cursor to End of Text', and click on OK.

3   Click on the far right in the 'Title' field. Have you noticed? The cursor jumps automatically to the end of 'Doctor', even when you click to the right of this (see Figure 17.11).

FIGURE 17.11   The cursor jumps automatically to the end of the text

4   Now open the OPTIONS dialog box, and switch off the option 'Position cursor to end of text'. Click on OK.

5   Click once more on the far right in the 'Title' field. This time the cursor remains where you click (see Figure 17.12).

FIGURE 17.12   The cursor stays where you click

The text in the input field is selected

1   You can try out this example too in the INITIAL ENTRY OF BASIC DATA window. Open the OPTIONS dialog box, CURSOR tab again.

2   Switch on the option 'Selecting the text in Edit field' and click on OK.

3   Set the cursor in the 'Form of address' field and press (Tab).

The text entered in the 'Title' field is automatically selected (see Figure 17.13).

FIGURE 17.13 The text is automatically selected

4 As soon as you enter text now, the entire former contents of the field are replaced by your new input. Try it out – just type any character.

How to set the cursor width

1 Once again, open the OPTIONS dialog box, CURSOR tab.
2 Under 'Cursor Width' you can specify the width of the displayed cursor (see Figures 17.14 and 17.15).

FIGURE 17.14 The narrow cursor looks like this...

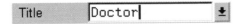

FIGURE 17.15 ...and the wide cursor like this

3 Do you still remember the information that is displayed in the status bar? Among other things, you can see there whether the data that you are entering is overwriting the existing data, or being inserted. If you switch on the option 'Block Cursor in Overwrite Mode', the switch between insert and overwrite will also be recognizable from the cursor. Switch on the option 'Block Cursor in Overwrite Mode', and click on OK.
4 Check whether the status bar shows OVW. If not, press the (Ins) key.
5 Set the cursor in the 'Title' field, for instance.

You can see from the cursor that existing data will be overwritten (see Figure 17.16).

FIGURE 17.16 For overwriting, the cursor is shown as a block

6 Press (Ins). You are thereby switching to insert mode, and the cursor once again appears as a vertical line.

COLOURS AND FONTS – WHATEVER YOU LIKE

Would you sometimes like to see your SAP R/3 window in other colours? Sample the possibilities SAP R/3 offers you. First of all, let's see how you can choose other colours for forms.

How to choose other colours for forms

1   Open the OPTIONS dialog box again.

2   Click on the tab page COLORS IN FORMS.

3   Choose a different colour palette from the colour palette list. A colour palette holds the colours for fields, texts in fields, etc. In this example we will try out the colour palette Orion (see Figure 17.17).

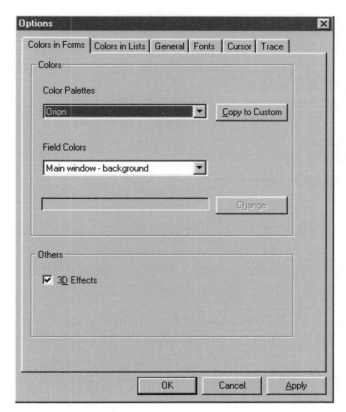

FIGURE 17.17   Choosing colour for forms

4 Click on OK.

The INITIAL ENTRY OF BASIC DATA window should still be open, so that you can see the change. Figure 17.18 shows the window with a different colour setting.

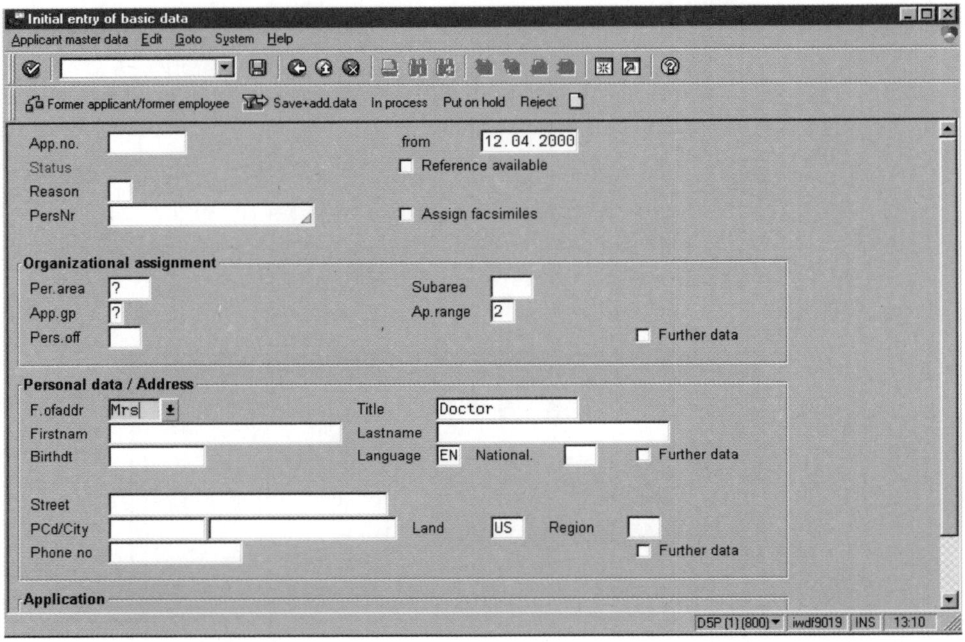

FIGURE 17.18 Different colours in forms

TIP   **YOU DON'T LIKE THE NEW COLOURS?**

If you don't like the new colours or you cannot read the data so well, it is easy to change them back. All you have to do is select the 'Standard' colour palette again.

If the available colour palettes do not appeal to you, you can also put together your own colours. You will find out more about that in the SAP R/3 Online help.

How to set a different font

1 The starting point is the OPTIONS dialog box. Click on the FONTS tab page.

2 Try them out and see which setting you like best. Have you noticed the preview in the window below? You can observe the effects of the font settings there (Figure 17.19).

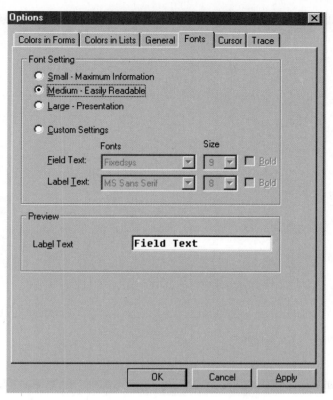

FIGURE 17.19   Set font

3   Once you have decided on a font, click on OK.

The next step is to try out the method for changing colours for lists.

How to choose different colours for lists

1   First we will create a list, so that there is something for you to see. Generate a report to look something like the one in Figure 17.20. Do this as you learned in Chapter 11.

2   Click on ⊡ (PAGE DISPLAY).

Your report is now presented as a list (Figure 17.21).

3   Now we will select a new colour for the column headers. Click on ⬤ and then on OPTIONS.

4   Click in the displayed dialog box on the COLORS IN LISTS tab page.

The dialog box should look like Figure 17.22.

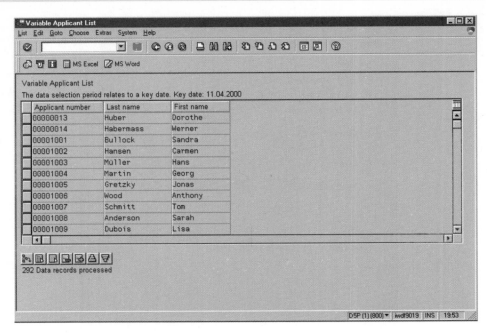

FIGURE 17.20 The starting point is a report

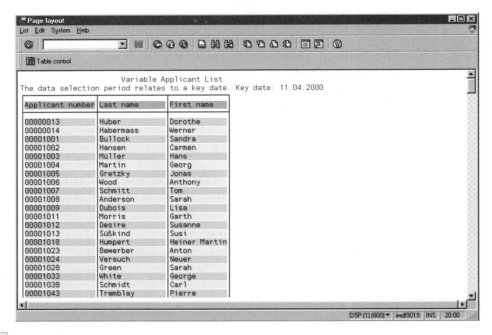

FIGURE 17.21 Report as list

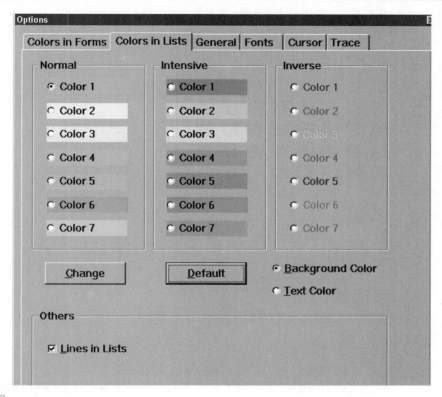

FIGURE 17.22   Choose colour for lists

5   Click under 'Intensive' on 'Color 1' and then on CHANGE.

6   Select a new colour in the displayed window. For this example we will take a light yellow (Figure 17.23).

7   Click on OK.

You return to the OPTIONS window. The colour you've just selected is now displayed under 'Intensive' as 'Color 1'. In this example it is light yellow.

8   Click on OK.

Figure 17.24 shows the new colour setting: The column headers now have a yellow background.

TIP   YOU DON'T LIKE THE NEW COLOUR?

It is very easy to convert the colours for lists to the standard setting again. Open the OPTIONS dialog box, COLORS IN LISTS tab. Click on STANDARD.

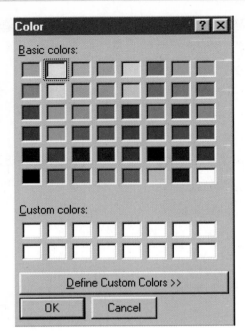

FIGURE 17.23 Pick a new colour

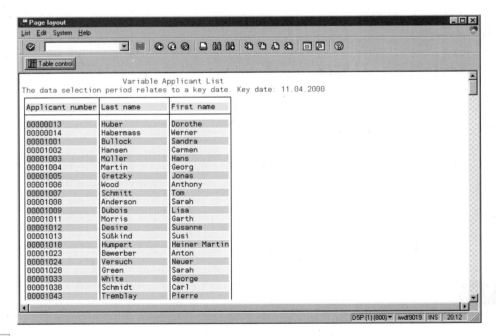

FIGURE 17.24 The new colours

9 Do you feel that the list has too many lines? That can be changed. Open the OPTIONS dialog box, COLORS IN LISTS tab once more.

10 Switch off the option 'Lines in Lists', and click on OK.

Figure 17.25 shows the result.

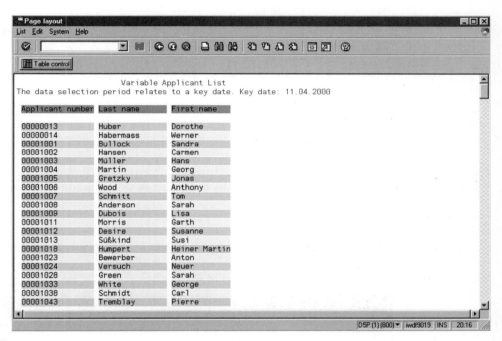

FIGURE 17.25 If you prefer lists without lines

TIP **WHERE ELSE DOES THE NEW LINE SETTING TAKE EFFECT?**

The option for display without lines also has a visual effect in tree structures. For example, look now at the report tree, which you saw in Section 11.4. This too is now displayed without lines. However, the structure does remain easily recognizable thanks to the indents.

SAP R/3 naturally offers you other options for styling your lists in your favourite colours. If we have made you curious, you can find further information in the SAP R/3 application help.

In this chapter you learned how to configure your working environment according to your wishes. This completes our tour of SAP R/3.

...And what next?

GuiXT

SAP R/3 has more to offer by way of support, and to make your work easier. For example, from Release 4.0 the program GuiXT is available free of charge as a component of the R/3 system. GuiXT makes it very easy to tailor the SAP R/3 user interface so that you can do your work still more easily and quickly. The possible adjustments include the following:

- Adding extra buttons to the button bar for functions that you often need
- Making windows easier to view by removing unnecessary fields from them
- Supporting orientation with separate illustrations
- Making operations easier with checkboxes
- And many more

These adjustments can easily be made by your own system administration. Ask your system administrator about GuiXT.

SAP AG on the Internet

Do you have access to the Internet? Then do visit the SAP AG website (Figure 17.26). You will find the latest information, notes about events, and much more relating to SAP AG under *http://www.H sap.com.*

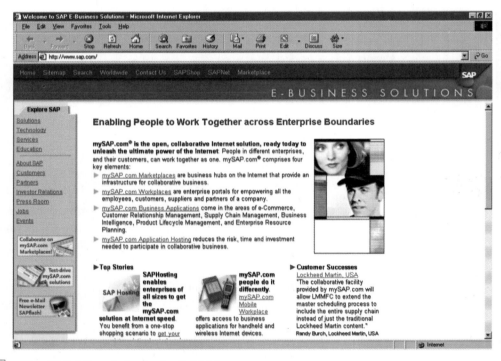

FIGURE 17.26 The SAP AG website in April 2000

SAPNet

A further important source of information is *SAPNet*: the communication medium by which SAP exchanges information with partners and customers. *SAPNet* doesn't just supply information on SAP, their services and products: you can also use it to order information, register for courses, etc.

To be able to make use of the *SAPNet*, you need a special user name (R/3 OSS user name) and a password. System administration will give you the user name and password for the initial logon. Why not find out about it?

So enjoy SAP R/3 – all the best as you work, learn and play!

Symbols in the standard toolbar

The table below lists the symbols that appear in the standard toolbar, with a description of what they do and the menu function/key combination required to implement them.

TABLE A.1 Meaning of the symbols in the standard toolbar

Symbol	Description	Menu function / key combination
✔ ENTER	Confirms the inputs made in the window. SAP R/3 checks the inputs. If all the necessary details are present and no errors are found, the next window can be displayed. Otherwise an error message is displayed.	(Return)
💾 SAVE	Checks whether the input data is error-free, complete and consistent. If so, the data is saved. Otherwise, an error message is displayed.	(F11) or EDIT | SAVE
⬅ BACK	In the initial window of an application: Returns to the application area menu. In a detail window of the application: Returns to the initial window.	(F3)

EXIT/LOG OFF/EXIT SESSION	In an application: Terminates the application and displays the previous menu level. In the logon window: Corresponds to a logoff from SAP R/3. At main menu level: Terminates the session.	(F15)
CANCEL	Cancels the current application. The entered data is not saved. If you have entered data, you will be asked if you really want to cancel the application.	(F12) or EDIT | CANCEL
PRINT	Prints the data in the current window.	(Ctrl) + (P)
FIND	Enables the search for a character string. Usually only available in reports.	(Ctrl) + (F)
FIND NEXT	Used for continuing the search for a character string. Usually only available in reports.	(Ctrl) + (G)
FIRST PAGE	Scrolls to the first page. Usually only available in reports.	(F21) or (Ctrl) + (PgUp)
PREVIOUS PAGE	Scrolls one page back. Usually only available in reports.	(F22) or (PgUp)
NEXT PAGE	Scrolls one page forward. Usually only available in reports.	(F23) or (PgDn)
LAST PAGE	Scrolls to last page. Usually only available in reports.	(F24) or (Ctrl) + (PgDn)
FIELD HELP	Displays help text for the current field.	(F1)
NEW SESSION	Opens a further session.	SYSTEM | CREATE SESSION
NEW SHORTCUT	Generates a new shortcut on your Windows desktop.	| GENERATE SHORTCUT

Glossary

ABAP ABAP is the language in which SAP R/3 is largely programmed. Many applications and reports are ABAP programs.

Application With the help of applications, you perform business or programming operations. You can call an application from a menu, or a shortcut on the Windows desktop, or by inputting the transaction code.

Application area Application area denotes the SAP R/3 functional range necessary for processing a subject area. This includes transactions, applications and windows.

Application toolbar see Button bar

Background processing In background processing, data is processed in the background while other functions can be executed in parallel on screen. The processing is not visible on screen.

Business process A business process describes a business flow within the company. This uses resources and can cut across departmental boundaries. When a business process is executed, the services of several cost centres of a controlling area may be enlisted.

Button A button is an element of the graphical user interface. By clicking on a button, you can call the function linked to the button. A button can be in graphic form, and/or labelled.

Buttons are also called *Pushbuttons*.

Button bar The button bar is an element of the graphical user interface. It is displayed in windows below the standard toolbar, and contains buttons with text and/or symbols, with which you can call applications. In contrast to the standard toolbar, the button bar changes depending on the chosen application area.

The button bar is also called the *Application toolbar.*

Cascading menu Cascading menus (submenus) are control elements of the graphical user interface. A cascading menu is a menu that is contained in another menu, and contains menu options itself. Cascading menus are indicated by small right triangles.

Checkbox Checkboxes are elements of the graphical user interface. Checkboxes are displayed when you can choose as many elements as you wish from a list of elements.

Client A client is a self-contained unit in terms of commercial law, organization and data. Several clients can be administered within an R/3 system.

Clipboard The clipboard can be used for temporary storage of character strings. It is used as a temporary storage area when copying and cutting data.

Cursor The cursor is a blinking vertical line that indicates where in the window your keyboard inputs will take effect.

Dialog box A dialog box is a window that is called from another window and displayed in that window. The inputs in the dialog box are used to support the main action that is taking place in the underlying window. Some dialog boxes must be closed before work can be resumed in the underlying main window.

F1 help   see Field help

Field help   Field help displays information about fields. The field help is called from the corresponding field.

Field help is also called F1 help because it can be called with the (F1) key.

Graphical user interface   The graphical user interface is the interface for controlling programs. In contrast to command-oriented interfaces, there is no need to enter commands: you can choose the commands you want with elements of the graphical user interface such as menus or symbols.

GUI   Abbreviation for Graphical User Interface.

Icon   see Symbol

Logon   During logon, your access rights for working with SAP R/3 are checked with your user name and password.

Main menu level   The main menu level is the top menu level of the SAP R/3 system. The main menu level contains a menu that is uniform throughout SAP, which the user obtains directly after logon. All the application areas offered by SAP are listed in the menu bar of the main menu level.

Mandatory Field   A required entry field is a field that must be filled in order that the data can be processed. Required entry fields are identified by a question mark.

Matchcode   A matchcode is a search criterion that can be used for finding records. All records that satisfy the entered search criterion are displayed as a result of the search.

Menu   A menu is a control element of the graphical user interface, and is used for choosing functions. One such function can be to open a cascading menu (submenu).

Menu bar   The menu bar is an element of the graphical user interface. The menu bar is below the title bar in a window.

Menu option   A menu option is an element of a menu. A menu option can be a function or a cascading menu.

Module   The components of SAP R/3, such as HR (Human resources management) or MM (Materials management), are also called modules.

Password   The password is a sequence of letters, digits or special characters, which you must give along with your user name when logging on. Your right to access the system is checked by means of the user name and password.

Pushbutton   see Button

Quick info   Quick info is the name for the text that is displayed when you point with the mouse pointer at a symbol in a standard toolbar. The quick info names the function that is called with the symbol, and the key combination that can alternatively be used to call this function.

Radio button   A radio button is an element of the graphical user interface, with which you can choose exactly one element from a list of elements.

Report   A report is the result of executing an ABAP report. When you start a report, the corresponding report program is executed. This involves reading and evaluating the data in the database tables. You can either display a report on screen or output it to a printer. You can also save the report, so that you can display it as often as you wish.

Search help   see Matchcode

Session A session is a window in which a particular task function can be processed. The system opens the first session during the logon to the R/3 system. You can open further sessions. Up to nine sessions can be open simultaneously. The number of the current session is displayed in the status bar.

Shortcut on the Windows desktop A shortcut is a symbol on the Windows desktop with which you can call an application. Double-click on the symbol to do so.

Standard toolbar The standard toolbar is an element of the graphical user interface.

The standard toolbar is below the menu bar in a window, and contains symbols for the basic SAP R/3 functions such as SAVE, as well as navigation and help functions.

Start screen see Start window

Start window The start window is the window that is displayed directly after logon.

Symbol A symbol is an element of the graphical user interface. By clicking on the symbol you can call the function linked to the symbol.

Symbols are sometimes also known as *Icons*.

Title bar The title bar is a component of a window, and shows the name of the window.

Transaction A transaction is a logical process in SAP R/3. From the user's point of view, a transaction is a self-contained unit (e.g. generate a list of certain customers, change the address of a customer, book a flight reservation for a customer, execute a program). You can display the initial window of a transaction either by choosing the appropriate menu options, or by double-clicking on a shortcut on the desktop, or by entering the transaction code.

Transaction code The transaction code is a sequence of characters that identifies a SAP transaction. When a transaction code is entered in the command field, the corresponding transaction is called in the R/3 system. For example, the transaction code SM31 denotes the transaction 'Table maintenance'.

User name Your user name is a character sequence by which you are known in the system. User names are set up by system administration.

Value help The value help shows the possible input values for a field. You can see whether there is value help for a field when you put the cursor in the field. If a downward arrow is shown beside the field, there is value help for this field.

Window A window is an element of the graphical user interface, and is used for data input or output. A window consists of the following elements: menu bar, title bar, standard toolbar, button bar, work area with fields, status bar.

Windows are sometimes also called *screens*.

Index

6696